The Advanced Pet Gundog

A common sense approach to gundog training

Lez Graham

Published by Trained for Life.
Copyright © Lez Graham.

First published by Trained for Life October 2011
ISBN 978-0-9570051-0-5

Photographs by Nick Ridley.
Printed and bound in Great Britain.

A catalogue record for this book is available from the British Library.

Contents

This book is dedicated to all of those, who like me,
share their home with a glorious gundog

Foreword

Over the years I have been lucky enough to watch some of the best gundog handlers and trainers in the country and as a keen "amateur" I am like a sponge when it comes to picking up new ideas and methods to make my training more successful.

I have had the pleasure of taking the pictures for both The Pet Gundog and now The Advanced Pet Gundog and I am sure Lez got sick and tired of me keep asking "why do you do that exercise that way I have never seen it done like that before?" Once Lez had kindly taken the time to explain to me the thought process behind the method, it was like a light bulb coming on!

As gundog trainers we know what WE want the dog to do but we very rarely give any thought as to what the DOG thinks we want it to do and therein lies the key to Lez's training methods.

Because of her vast experience as a dog behaviourist she understands what makes a dog tick and it is this knowledge that she applies in her training and she willingly shares in The Advanced Pet Gundog.

I have quite a large collection of gundog training books and not one of them have any mention of what a dog can see in terms of colour or how the dog's scenting mechanism works and yet surely we should have an understanding of those two abilities as it enables us to understand why a dog can't seem to find what on the face of it seems like a simple retrieve.

I am so pleased that Lez has included these two factors in this book and I for one found it fascinating and it has given me another excuse to use when my dog can't find an orange dummy!

Nick Ridley

Acknowledgements

In the same way it takes a community to raise a child, I believe that it takes family and friends, and not just the author, to write a book.

In some ways I've found this second book much easier to write than my first, partly because I knew what I was doing and letting myself in for and partly because my husband and the people around me knew what they were letting themselves in for too... In other ways it was more challenging as it's a much more technical book and trying to find the words to explain how to do things caused many sleepless nights and early mornings.

I was also doing my Masters degree alongside it which was a mammoth task in itself and kept pulling me away from what I wanted to focus on which was completing this book, however, it was a really interesting thing to do and I'm so glad that I did it, especially as it has had an impact on how I train. Again, it wasn't just me who put the effort in for my masters and led to subsequent knowledge gained; it was all of those involved on the day and who took part in the experiment.

And so, on behalf of not only myself, but from future gundog trainers and their dogs, great thanks is given to Kenny Graham and Ross McCarthy for filming the experiment and providing evidence for change, and to my handlers with their dogs, without whom the experiment wouldn't have taken place; Alexandra Jackson Kay with Lily, Charlotte Hitchmough with Topo, Darren Burbidge with Moss, Gae Moore with Tolla, Jill Thorpe with Poppy and Fern, Sally Cockcroft with Beanie, Stephen Williams with Peter and Jack, and last but not least, Titus O'Brien with Sandy.

Much appreciation goes once more to Nick Ridley, not only for the superb photos and designing the front cover, but for also writing the foreword; to The Countryside Alliance for granting me permission to resurrect an out of print poster; to Sue Jackson at Quest Gundog Training Equipment for supplying me with dummies and the like, and also to Ian and Jill Clinton of The Working Dog Company for supplying me with their innovative and award winning rugby ball shaped dummies.

My gratitude goes to Jill Stagg for always being there to bounce things off and to Peter Stagg for helping me get my head around, and write, the section on the pheasant shoot; as it does to Charlotte, Darren, Nick and Sally for once again allowing me to include photos of their gorgeous gundogs; Topo the Spanish Water Dog, Moss the Labrador Retriever, Harry the Working Cocker Spaniel and Beanie the English Springer Spaniel.

Great thanks must be afforded to 'the gundoggers' who train with me week in week out, in rain, wind, sun, snow and rain. If you remember it rains a lot on gundog days which is why I always mention it twice. They have taught me so much over the years - not least that, even though I'm their gundog trainer, me and my dogs don't have to be perfect at everything... only most things.

And finally, I owe once again the greatest debt to my husband for not complaining about the restless nights as I wrestled with the words in my head, for the endless proof reading and spell checking and for making me laugh; especially in his translation of the title whilst mimicking my native Geordie tongue – "Why it's The Advanced Gundog, Pet".

Introduction

Originally I was going to write one big book entitled The Pet Gundog which covered gundog training from choosing your puppy to going on a shoot.

However, not only was it a truly daunting task but I thought that the majority of pet gundog owners really don't want anything more than a very well behaved dog that they can take for walks and enjoy throwing things for in a relatively structured way; I know when I first started out with gundogs this is all I wanted - the thought of picking up a dead bird used to fill me with dread.

Times change though as do people; I've found, for myself and also for the people that I train, that the more we are involved in the shooting world and go shooting, the more we want to be involved in the shooting world and go shooting. There's something very primal and satisfying about the shoot, maybe it's because you feel a part of something bigger, the cycle of life and all of that, or maybe it's just because it's a great day out in the fresh air with like minded people. All I know is that the more you embrace the shooting world the more you want to embrace it.

Likewise, people who have an adult dog at home don't necessarily want to read about toilet training and puppy training and so it was back to the proverbial drawing board to split my idea up into more manageable chunks to write and also make more appealing to the gundog owner.

And so was born a set of three gundog training books for the pet gundog owner:

The Pet Gundog introduced you to the psychology of the dog as well as how to achieve a well-behaved and well-mannered dog at home. Basic training was covered as was basic gundog training; enough to get your pet gundog retrieving nicely and doing a bit of hunting. We dipped our toes into the shooting world, enough so that you could understand what your dog had been bred for and how to exploit that breeding.

This book, The Advanced Pet Gundog, picks up where The Pet Gundog leaves off and will take you from the basic retrieve to a shoot, if that's what you'd like to do with your dog, to the Working Gundog Certificate or a Novice Working Test... well, the techniques and 'how to' are covered anyway; the rest, as they say, is up to you.

The final book as you may guess, is The Pet Gundog Puppy which will start with "can I have a puppy?" through to the young dog being 8 months old and embarking on more advanced training.

As with all of my books, The Advanced Pet Gundog is not group specific, by that I mean it will cover the training for all round retrieving and hunting... not quite a 'one size fits all' but not far off - HPR and Setter specific training are not covered.

Any specialised techniques should really be worked through with a trainer rather than going for a distance learning approach, which is what training via a book is, however, saying that, if you persevere and practice your training little and often, there's no reason why great things can't be achieved.

And now, it's time to roll up our sleeves and get on with some training!

Gundog 101

Before we get on with the serious business of extending our dogs' (and our) learning, first we have to have a little look and see not only what we've done so far, but whether we're happy with what we've done so far.

You can't have a well-trained, bad-mannered dog; that's not strictly true, you can and in the past I have, however, it's really not a good look and so we'll be assessing behaviour in a second as well as training.

My first lab, Bart, was a really well-trained gundog when we first moved to New Zealand in 2004, however, he wasn't overly well-mannered – we used to call him Bargy Bart; that is until I met behaviourist Noel Hutchinson, whose first words to me were "your dog has atrocious manners". He was right of course, at that time I put more emphasis on training rather than behaviour and spent more time controlling my dogs rather than teaching them self control, no more though. Although you can have one without the other, the question has to be "why would you want to?"

Many hours were spent outside of competition obedience rings watching these dogs do amazingly complex pieces of obedience, only to drag their handlers out of the rings and go tanking up to all and sundry demanding sweeties and scratches; how much nicer it would have looked if the dogs had just padded alongside their handlers, hanging out with them after having a good time strutting their stuff. So, as well as advanced training we're also looking for impeccable manners.

In the past when I've read a trilogy, or a longer series of books, it would irritate me that the first couple of chapters were devoted to setting the plot and summarising the preceding books; by the time I got to the new story I'd turned off and was thinking of what else I could read. I thought I would take a different approach...

So here we go; gundog 101. Look on the following more as a self assessment and bit of self reflection rather than a test, unless of course you enjoy tests - in which case you're in for a treat; this is a biggie!

Can your dog do this?

When you choose to share your life (and home) with a dog, regardless of breed, they have to be well-mannered; at home, in the car and outside. It should be the norm rather than the exception, expected rather than begged for.

The following are basic good manners that were covered within The Pet Gundog and should really be a part of your dog's makeup by the time you're ready to embark upon more advanced gundog training...

Long time no see!

When you come home or haven't seen your dog for a little while does he run around like the Tasmanian devil, bouncing about you, jumping up and barking or is he composed or excited but respectful?

My dogs are always happy to see me, however, they're respectful with their exuberance and if I'm carrying shopping or have my hands full they never try to get in the thick of it, nosing whatever I have or being bargy. They respect my space and if they forget themselves for a moment, a look or an 'ah-ah', will soon having them minding their manners again.

That doesn't mean there's not great excitement when we get together, it just means I choose when it's going to happen not them, and that's generally after I've unpacked the grocery shopping or taken off coats and boots or made a cuppa.

After you...

Do you tell your dog to sit and wait when you approach a door or does he automatically take a step back? If you tell him to sit then you're controlling his behaviour through training rather than your dog displaying self control around a more important animal – you.

If this is the case you really need to revisit the section on doorway manners within The Pet Gundog - doorways are such an important thing, not just for dogs but for us also. We would never dream of barging past a more important person, any person really, just to get through the door first. To do so is the height of bad manners and parents will chastise youngsters for it and if it's an adult that does it they'd more than likely be tutted at or have a sarcastic remark thrown at them.

I don't know if you've read or seen Harry Potter and The Half Blood Prince, but there's a great bit in it where Harry and Ron can take Potions but neither of them have a potions book. Off they go to the store cupboard where there are two books left; a brand spanking new one and a tatty old one falling apart at the seams. Immediately there's a competition between them to see who can get to the new book first and guess where it takes place...

You've got it, in the doorway – all the barging and pushing takes place at the threshold to the store cupboard, the first one through the door is the victor.

Need I say more?

May I start?

As with doorways you can either control your dog by 'telling' him to sit-stay/sit-wait for his food or you can instil good manners so that he doesn't attempt to touch the food until you allow him; no commands necessary - you put the food down silently, he waits, you release, he eats.

If you're doing sit-stays prior to feeding you're controlling your dog's behaviour rather than him controlling his own. Although reading this you may feel as if it's splitting hairs, it really isn't; I can't stress enough how important self control is for a gundog, especially around food.

Remember you're about to embark on advanced gundog training and that means, if you decide to go shooting, that your dog will have to exercise enough self control to bring back and place in your hand a bloody but alive bird, rabbit or anything else you point him at.

Congratulations, if you've given yourself an A you have a well mannered and deferential gundog sharing your life....

If however, when reading the above you've thought "hmmm, not really" you need to seriously consider going back to the beginning of The Pet Gundog, gaining an understanding of how your dog thinks and apply the good manners section until you and your dog are at the appropriate level. To embark on advanced gundog training whilst your dog is not respecting you or looking to you for leadership is to give yourself a much more difficult job than you need to.

Okay, so you got an A, fantastic - well done you. Now the question you need to ask yourself is how well trained is he?

Can your dog do that?

Walking to heel
It really doesn't matter which side your dog walks on, although as you know it is to do with your 'dominant' hand; what matters is that when on lead your dog doesn't pull and when off lead your dog isn't dawdling, drifting or meandering around with his nose on the ground.

Doing nothing
Doing nothing is just that, doing nothing. When you stop and relax so should your dog. If you're in the middle of a field, the busy high street or watching your kids play football, when you do nothing it's a chance for your dog to relax by your side, hang out with you, his leader, and learn to be comfortable in his own skin.

If your dog is constantly trying to pick things up, stretching to the end of his lead and be a general pain in the nether regions then you really need to work on this exercise - it will pay dividends when you go shooting.

Meeting and greeting
Can you stop and chat to someone in the street or on a walk without your dog turning into a yobbo? Does he chill out beside you either sitting or lying relaxing or is he straining at the lead to see the other dog or jumping all over the owner?

Guess which one you're aiming for? You really don't want to cover the gamekeeper or the guns in mud and slobber the first, or even any time, you turn up for the shoot.

Recall
Does your dog come when called? When either using the whistle or verbally calling him? Both should work equally and by that I don't mean equally poorly - I mean both whistle and voice get an automatic response from your dog of turning on the spot and getting back to you as fast as physically possible.

If you're in any doubt then you haven't got a reliable recall and please go back and train it; to have a dog without a recall is a time bomb waiting to off...

Overly dramatic? I think not; I had a phone call from a lady a couple of days ago whose poodle would stay away for 20-30 minutes at a time, if he was with a certain dog he was known to be gone for 3 hours at a time - how many accidents could that dog have caused? In the country (which is where she is) the dogs could have worried sheep making the ewes reabsorb lambs and worse; I've known 'plains dogs' have fun reverting to type tearing apart foxes and killing sheep.

Sit

Does your dog sit when told? If the answer is no, there's absolutely no point whatsoever in continuing reading. Do yourself and your dog a favour, and save you both some stress, and go back and do some serious basic training.

Remember that when you do your basic training, you are in effect, putting in the foundations for the more advanced training. You could liken it to learning the ABC's - you wouldn't go from reading the Peter and Jane books straight onto Lord of the Rings – you'd work your way through The Cat in the Hat, The Famous Five and Harry Potter first.

Whistle sit

Is your dog sitting on the whistle every time? Including at distance? If he is, fantastic, he'll need to be able to for the advanced training you're about to embark upon, if he's not, start training it from today on your daily walks so that by the time you get to the part of the book where we use it your dog will be ready.

Stay

If your dog cannot do a sit (or down) stay for more than a couple of minutes it's time to do some serious training. A stay is such an important exercise to train, not just important but vital.

Let's just say you're in the field and need to get across a fence; you put your dog over first and tell him to sit-stay whilst you clamber across, he's been well trained and waits while you unhook yourself from the wire, find your balance, go back for your stick and so on. Perfect.

What about if you hadn't trained him? You put your dog over first and tell him to sit-stay whilst you clamber across, he gets a bit bored waiting while you unhook yourself from the wire, finds a scent and runs headlong towards the beating line as he can hear the beaters and wants to be part of it; you're left hooked up onto the fence, going scarlet in the face from repeatedly blowing on the whistle, screaming after your dog and utter embarrassment.

Know which scene I'd rather see myself in!

Leave it

Will your dog turn his head away from an object of desire when you say 'leave it'? Will he relinquish an object of desire when you tell him to 'leave it', 'give' it, 'drop' it or 'dead'?

There is absolutely no point in going any further with the training unless he does; you're about to make life very interesting for your dog, enjoyable and exciting, if he doesn't turn away or give things up now, before that happens, then when he gets a dressed dummy in his mouth you're going to have to prise his jaws apart – that's presuming he'll come back to you with 'his prize'.

So, how did you get on?

If your dog can't successfully do the above on command then you need to think about whether that's affecting his behaviour and training.

A lot of times a recall problem is indicative of a lack of leadership at home; if for example you have to tell your dog to sit five times, go on his bed five times and so on, he's learning that the first four commands you give you don't mean – why therefore, should he come back first time you tell him to?

Remember that every time you interact with your dog you're training on one level or another... the thing you're training him could just as easily be to ignore you as to obey you.

Taking it to the next level

Although I talked canine psychology in The Pet Gundog, it was more of an introduction to it rather than an encyclopedia and so throughout this book we'll be getting inside our dog's heads as much as we possibly can; after all how can we develop any kind of relationship with our dog, working or otherwise, if we don't understand him, see the world as he sees it (or at least try to) and have some sort of inkling as to what makes him tick.

I find it such a privilege to work with dogs; to have that bond and understanding. Crossing the species barrier is just wonderful and seeing what motivates them (or turns them off) in different situations. Sometimes, the instinct may be so strong to do something, that no manner of rewards are going to do it for them (technically called the instinctual drift), other times the focus and motivation is so strong you can almost feel your dogs eyes boring into you, desperately trying to get you to do their bidding.

One of the many things to remember, and in some ways as a dog trainer and owner, the most important, is that if you want your dog to change, first of all you must; you must be the change you want to see in your dog.

Your behaviour shapes your dog's behaviour

Let's just say for example you've had a hard day at work, you've come home, given your dog a stroke and you're now sitting on the settee watching telly with your dinner on your lap. You've got your dog with you and told him to go on his bed as you come in the room. By the time you're sitting down your dog is half on and half off his bed; what do you do?

Well, if you ignore him, before you know it he'll be off his bed and either wandering around, begging and drooling over your dinner, or if you're lucky, lying at your feet. *You told him to go on his bed and you're not reinforcing it.* But what you are reinforcing however, is that you don't actually mean what you say and the dog can choose to ignore you. Not a biggie do I hear you think? True, but not great when you apply that same logic to the recall, retrieve and any one of a hundred commands that you want your dog to do immediately and without hesitation.

If you'd put your dog back on his bed as soon as he got up you would be telling him that you mean what you say and more importantly you're willing to back it up; that he can't get away with paying lip-service or only half completing what you've asked of him *and* that you expect him to do as he's told first time.

That doesn't mean getting all growly with him over it, just put him back on his bed and tell him he's a good boy once he's there and lying down – if he goes to get up just 'ah-ah' him and tell him to "go on your bed".

I trained my dogs to go on their beds using first of all Shapes, then Bonios (in order to keep them on their beds for a little longer whilst they ate). Once they'd finished eating I would give them the release command so they were free to go. Oh, by the way, for me 'on your bed' means go and lie down on your bed – standing on it just doesn't cut it... he must be lying down. I then increased the amount of time between them finishing eating and releasing them. Whenever we eat in the living room the dogs are in there on their beds before we even get in the room, waiting and drooling for their biscuit - they know they can't get off until we say so and so they turn their backs on us and go to sleep once they've finished.

In the early days though, I cannot tell you the amount of times I had to put my plate down and lead my youngster by his collar back to his bed. If there's more than one of you at home take turns with this exercise, if you're on your own don't expect a hot dinner for a few days. With a dog that is learning this exercise, young or old, use his collar and 'escort' him back, however, once your dog knows the command and what it means and is just pushing the boundaries, then use the herding method to put him back.

Once you've trained your dog to do something, then regardless of what it is, he should be doing it first time, every time. Remember that if you tell your dog to do something that he knows how to do (and you know he knows because you've trained him to do it) and he doesn't do it, then he's making a choice, and that choice is to ignore you. He's basically decided you're not important enough for him to do your bidding and will do his own thing instead.

If your dog is not working for you he is working for himself. If he's working for himself he's making choices. If he's making choices he's taking control. If he's taking control then he's in charge and if he's in charge... you're not!

Handing over your power

I remember a few years ago when I was running the Kennel Club's Good Citizen Award Scheme at a local village hall, one of my handlers would have terrible trouble with her very strong Labradoodle. I'd often seen them walking through town whilst I was in the car and he was impeccably behaved, walking nicely on the lead and just padding alongside his owner.

When he came into the village hall however, he turned into a Jekyll and Hyde dog and used to bounce around, pull, bark and generally be a pain in the proverbial. Then one day the penny dropped. His owner was a strong capable lady who knew her own mind and tended to get on with things, however, when she came to training she was a pupil and handed over her power to me – her dog felt it and played her up.

The solution?

I had her take the class for one exercise. She took control of everyone in the hall and everyone did as they were told, including her dog; never again did she relinquish her power as she stepped through the door and never again did her dog mess her about.

Good dog, sick dog, soft dog syndrome

I try to look upon raising dogs in the same way as raising children; set boundaries at home, enforce them and nurture your child within them, encouraging good manners and success at things that interest them and frowning upon bad manners and bad behaviour.

One of the many great things that happen as a result of taking control of your household is that your dog (and your child) relaxes and stops seeking or demanding attention. Things become so much more chilled and relaxed and your dog becomes a joy to have around.

The down side of this is that you start to relax the discipline and the rules and before you know it you have a demanding pushy gundog again (known in the behaviour trade as 'good dog syndrome').

Not only should you be aware of 'good dog' syndrome as described above, but you need to be on the lookout for 'sick dog' syndrome also. Yup you got it, your dog's a bit poorly and you baby him. Who can blame you?

Not me that's for sure, I'm terrible at babying my dogs when they're not well and spend my evenings lying on the floor cuddling them, giving them head and neck massages and generally fussing over them, however, even while I'm babying them I do it as their leader not as someone paying homage to them as a lower rank would do, which means insisting they don't clamber all over me uninvited and when I go to get up they get off me and move away. The quickest way to undo all the great stuff you've done in instilling good manners will be to give your dog lots and lots of privileges.

Always remember that if you can't, or won't, enforce a command then don't give it; this is especially true with a sick dog.

So that's good dog and sick dog but what about soft dog? Well, Angus my Goldie is a soft dog, as is my youngster Ziggy; very soft, the pair of them. Hard to believe when you see Ziggy's hackles travel from the nape of his neck, across his shoulders and half way down his tail, but a soft dog he is.

Because they're soft does that mean that they're not determined and strong willed? No not at all.

My youngster is still very much developing his personality and being rounded out, but Angus is now six and a half and is about to go into his fourth picking up year. Although he's not very bold but can be quite brave and will try things if I ask him to but he never puts himself forward; he needs soft but strong handling.

Soft as in; I can't get angry or raise my voice as he would crumple, any displays of frustration on my part (and there have been many, many frustrating moments with Angus) and he would switch off completely and either lie down or snatch at the grass.

Strong as in; if I don't act as if I know what I'm doing he wanders off and does his own thing, likewise if no clear boundaries are set then he develops selective deafness and turns his back on everyone, or, if I don't give clear commands when working him, he stands still and looks at me as if I've never given him a day's training in his life; you can almost hearing him thinking "nope, you've not taught me that, uh-uh, not seen that one before".

Soft dogs need leaders as much as strong dogs do, they just need careful handling, and for that the rewards are vast as you see your less than bold dog doing things you never in a million years expected them to achieve.

Motivating the unmotivated – you and the dog...

Unfortunately with the advent of dressing dogs up, handbag dogs and designer mongrels (for example the cockapoo and springador), we've stopped seeing the dog for what it really is; an animal, a predator and which has all the drives and instincts of one. Once we remember that the dog is a dog and start treating him as such we'll find a million and one ways to motivate him.

Okay that was a slight exaggeration but we'll certainly find a few. Before we look at motivation though, we first need to remind ourselves what it means to be a dog: dogs have no morals, ethics or principles. Domestication doesn't remove the survival instinct it just dulls it slightly; smoothing off the rough edges.

Dogs still live within the law of the animal kingdom which is survival of the fittest; it really is a dog eat dog world out there. They have no concept of cannibalism or rape; if they want to eat it they will if they can and if they want to sexually mount something and they can, then they will.

I can remember years ago walking across Croydon shopping centre on the way to the train station for work and seeing a couple of pigeons tucking in to some KFC and thinking 'oh gross cannibalism or what' I then caught myself pondering over it whilst sitting on the train when the realisation dawned; cannibalism is a humanism – in the animal kingdom it's called survival.

When you think about it, the retrieve is the hunt with the final element suppressed; there is the mark, the chase, no kill and then returning the prey back to the pack. This is why it's especially important that we are the most important thing and the most senior rank in our dog's world. I've seen many gundogs where it wasn't the case and the dog would run out, pick up a bird then go hide under a tree and eat it, becoming growly and aggressive with the owner if they tried to take it away.

Every relationship has someone that leads; whether that is within your parental family, a marriage, friendship, walking with someone, dancing with someone, working with someone – there is always one person that decides the pace of the relationship, the walk, the dance moves or what the priorities are. In human relationships this *leader* can change over time or circumstances. In your relationship with your dog that person (or animal) has got to be you, *always* – it is quite simply a disaster waiting to happen if it's not.

The majority of the motivation to please you will come from the fact that you are your dog's leader, however, you don't want your dog just tagging along because he has to; you want him to want to work for you and with you as well, and this is where the art of motivation comes in.

While we want to reward our dog with praise, a stroke and a smile, sometimes we need more and by this I mean either a food reward or playing with a toy. I do play pull or tug with my gundogs, if you train a good hold and a good release command it won't affect their mouth – Angus, my Goldie has one of the softest mouths I've come across and I've played pull with him since he was six or seven months old. A word of warning though with food training and the retrieve; don't do it... your dog knows he cannot possibly eat that yummy treat whilst he's got a bit of canvas in his mouth so he will get rid of the canvas and start spitting out the dummy – a behaviour trait you really don't want your dog to learn.

If your dog's not doing something right don't take it personally, have a think about whether you've really trained an exercise thoroughly enough for your dog to understand what you want him to do. Have you skipped a stage in his training? Have you jumped from 'A is for Apple' and the Peter and Jane books to Lord of The Rings, without stopping off at The Cat in the Hat and Winnie the Pooh? This is really common, especially with the brighter and more enthusiastic dogs. Slow down. Assess your training and training techniques, body language and voice tone before you become disheartened.

Keep your training light hearted and fun, that way you'll both enjoy it, and remember that, with a gundog, the reward is the retrieve and the retrieve should be rewarded. Any 'dicking about' however, whilst retrieving, should still be corrected; just carefully so as not to create any problems further down the road of training.

'Correction' doesn't mean getting angry with your dog and definitely not scragging, picking up, shaking, swinging around, beating, slapping around the face or any one of the many things I've witnessed gundog trainers (and owners) do over the years – it means applying a bit of common sense and employing the word that you've used since puppy days "NO!" or "AH-AH". To really understand discipline and my views on it though you need to read The Pet Gundog as I noted at the beginning of this book that I wasn't going to go over old ground.

Correction on its own won't work, but then again neither will praise on its own, especially when your dog gets it into his head that it is a game or that he can mess around and still get praised for doing so; in order for your dog to change you must use both. The motivation is to please you and be praised by *you* and avoid being frowned upon by *you*.

Be in the moment and only in the moment when you're training – you really cannot be anywhere else and if people talk to you mid exercise, complete the exercise first before responding otherwise your dog will pick up on the fact that you're distracted. The amount of times in training I say to my handlers "you don't have to tell me what your dog is doing, I can see for myself – focus on your dog and correct the behaviour". Funnily enough they never give me a running commentary when it's going right, only when it's going pear shaped, which, you've got it, will make it worse as the handler takes their focus off their dog and the dog, being a dog, takes full advantage of the situation.

Remember to praise your dog if he's doing well; he really can achieve an A+ for effort. If you're holding out for perfection before you give your dog any kind of praise or encouragement you'll be waiting an awfully long time; it's the praise and encouragement that will motivate your dog to improve upon what he's doing. If it goes badly, or not quite as you want it to, let it go; don't carry the baggage of a previous training session or exercise as that will affect how you approach what you're doing now.

Try to keep your emotions out of it and learn to bluff - even if you're at the end of your tether don't show it. Stay in the moment and try to complete the exercise on a high note. If that's not possible change the exercise so your dog succeeds and gains your approval, thereby ending the session on a good note.

A couple of weeks ago I did a Working Test with Angus (really not my thing as for me it's all about the training and working my dogs on a shoot, however, if I'm going to write about it I have to do it). It was one of those days where the rain is horizontal; you open your curtains, close them again and crawl back into bed. If I hadn't been going with a couple of handlers on their first working test that's exactly what I would have done, instead I put off going for my shower and then rushed around like a headless chicken – you know those kind of days.

Anyway, standing in torrential rain on a Sunday morning soaked to the skin (my 100% waterproof jacket was 100% waterproof for the first hour then became 100% waterlogged) just wasn't doing it for me and by the time we got to the fourth test, a retrieve in the forest, I was cold, very wet and had a severe case of the grumples. Sending Angus out for the blind, he kept air-scenting the dummies that the thrower had hanging in a tree and then running across the dummy in favour of the marked retrieve that went down first. After handling him back to the area a couple of times and feeling myself getting frustrated as I could feel the rain seeping up my cuffs and down my neck, I called him in and asked the judge if he could ask his assistant to re-throw the dummy so we could end the test 'successfully'.

Regardless of whether you're training, competing or competing for fun (if there is such a thing) you owe it to your dog to end on a high - even if it is a faked one.

That's not my training technique...

It can be very difficult learning how to do things from a book, which is why I tend to give lots of examples or share experiences, (rather than just write a technical book that says do this and do that) to try to highlight where things can go wrong as well as using photo sequences to illustrate how to do things correctly.

You can imagine my surprise (and horror) therefore, when a few months after The Pet Gundog came out someone came for a one to one with me and in order to get her dog to walk to heel she bent over the top of him, about turned, gave a wiggle with the lead and then about turned again after a stride, still bending over the dog and gave him a biscuit.

"That was interesting" I said "where did you learn that?" "Oh, I got it from your book" was her reply. "No you didn't, that's not in my book and please don't tell anyone it is" I said once I managed to get my jaw off the ground.

If you're going to use a technique from a book, and please do as there's some absolute crackers out there (and in here I hasten to add), please read and then read again before trying it out; if the technique doesn't work for you then read it through again, maybe get someone to video you and compare it with the technique that is written down – it may be a tiny thing that you're doing differently, but if the technique isn't working then you need to change it.

I hadn't really thought about creating a DVD although I've been asked many times to do one, however, after having a visit from this lady and her lovely black Labrador I'm seriously considering it.

Obedience

To me, gundogs are the most obedient, highly trained of all the pet dogs; or at least they should be anyway. When you think about it, as soon as you start to work your dog he's at a distance to you and, if you take him shooting, he'll be working under his own steam, finding things for you but still being under control. I can't think of any other discipline that requires such a high level of obedience; normally highly skilled obedience dogs are beside, or reasonably close to, their owners not working a couple of hundred feet away.

I've been asked many times if a pet gundog that lives indoors is going to be any use on a shoot; a resounding YES is always the reply. I know many people who have their gundogs living indoors and have an excellent working relationship with their dog. The training however, or rather the discipline involved in the training is different. The manner in how you go about your training is different too...

This section is, as you may have guessed, all about taking your obedience to the next level for both you and your pet gundog.

Steady Eddie

When you have a dog living indoors you have a million and one smells to compete with as well as all the fluffy toys, tennis balls and half eaten chewsticks to take into account.

You say to your dog 'do this' and the response can be anything from "yes boss, right away", to "were you talking to me?", "in a minute, I'm busy" or even... "   ". Okay, I'm doing the whole anthropomorphising thing but you get the idea don't you.

Once in the great outdoors, on lead or off, the last thing you want is a fired up gundog in his nose, running off every two minutes and totally disregarding you.

You want a dog that will just pad along beside you and only 'fire up' when you tell him to. This goes against what a lot of gundog trainers do, I know, but I fix many pet gundogs which have been trained by people who only know how to train outdoor dogs for field trials.

When you have a pet gundog you need to train steadiness before anything else; even with spaniels that traditionally were allowed to be in their noses until eight or nine months and then brought into line. For me, however, the last thing you need or want is an out of control spaniel; do yourself and your spaniel a favour and forget all about hunting with it until you've trained the basics, have a great recall and a fantastic retrieve as well as walking to heel on and off lead... *then* switch on his nose!

Fizz buzz, fizz buzz, buzz fizz

When you have a kennelled dog you are his excitement for the day. When you open the kennel door is when his day should brighten and oh boy is he ready to please you.

You want the dog to be all buzzy and fired up around you; you'll get him out of his kennel, maybe do a few minutes heelwork, then some retrieves or other gundog exercises, then it is back into the kennel for a few hours. The training is intense and will be done for short periods of time.

The dogs are so wired at the thought of training that they tend to be fizzy at the beginning of the session – they're returned to the kennel as they start to calm down as the training is normally done by then, thus the dog learns that being with the trainer is all about being on his toes, restraint needs to be shown yes, but they are still fizzy and, if he's a spaniel, then buzzing around legs or back and forth as fast as he can go is the order of the day.

This really is where training a pet gundog that lives indoors with you is a world apart from training a kennelled gundog. Most people, and I would have included myself years ago, are seriously impressed by the fizziness of the trialling dogs and go to trainers that train that way. Unfortunately it quite often unravels in the normal daily routine and walks of the pet dog and the owners quite often end up over-dogged with no idea how to put it right.

Car manners

Something that I was very impressed with when I went on my first shoot, was the fact that all of the dogs sat in the back of the car quite happily and quite quietly whilst the back was open. They didn't try to get out and for the most part, when they did they didn't mob anyone. Wow!

I've subsequently heard about a couple of dogs being killed when the lock on the car door came undone and the back window/door opened and the dog got out. Having not been told to stay the dogs just jumped out... straight into the paths of cars and trailers.

In The Pet Gundog you were taught how to stop a dog barging past you out of a doorway. You're going to expand that technique to stop your dog jumping out of the car without permission, so rather than your dog thinking he can jump out unless you say otherwise (stay, no etc.,) he's now going to think that unless you say otherwise (out, come on then etc.,) he's not allowed out of the car.

The same applies if your dog travels in a crate

Before you start make sure your windows are clean, as you want to be able to easily see your dog, if you can't see him you could hurt him by not reacting quickly enough. With your dog in the back of your car (leave the lead on to start off with), start to open the door ever so slowly; as soon as your dog starts to move, noisily close the door. Keep doing this until your dog backs away from the door. As you open it pretend to close it, *NEVER TAKING YOUR EYES OFF YOUR DOG*. Once it's open you can employ the 'not you' command if it gives you more confidence.

To start off with I wouldn't make your dog stay still for very long, quite literally a second or two after managing to open the door all the way release your dog. Build it up so that you can stand in front of him for a minute or so then start standing to the side for a couple of seconds. Remember every time you increase the complexity of an exercise you reduce the duration or the distance.

Please only do this when you know it would be safe for your dog to jump out, for example in a secure driveway or a garage. I cannot stress enough that you should never take your eyes off the dog when pretending to close the door as you don't want to catch him.

Other than employing the 'not you' command, if you feel the need, until you release your dog you should be silent.

Recall

In The Pet Gundog we trained the recall for your dog to come and sit in front which was the precursor if you like, for a nice delivery to hand. Now we're going to move it forward and train your dog to come straight to heel on the whistle, regardless of whether you're on the move or standing still.

If you want your dog to come in front of you, for example when he's presenting, that's absolutely fine; you'll still have your 'come' command so you can use your whistle recall and then, when he's about ten feet in front of you say "come" and move your hands in front of you at your tummy as you have always done.

Whistle to heel whilst stationary

Pop your dog in a 'sit-wait' and walk about 20 paces away from him. Just before you turn to face him put your whistle in your mouth and a sweetie in your left hand.

Face your dog, give the recall whistle and smile. When your dog is between six and ten feet away from you, put your left hand forward so that you're luring your dog to your left and do the 'finishing' sequence that you've already perfected; you know the left leg back and luring your dog through an anti-clockwise circle ending with a sit by your left leg. As you do so, say "heel". It won't take long for your dog to realise that when you blow the recall whistle it's his job to come back as fast as possible and do a 'hand-brake turn' into the heel position.

In time you'll be able to keep your legs still and just lure him round.

whistle your dog...

...then lure him round...

...and using a treat guide him into the heel position

Whistle to heel on the move

You won't always be standing still when you whistle your dog to heel, at least it will be highly unlikely anyway; for the most part you'll be on the move.

With your dog on a lead, and it needs to be a fairly long lead, 6ft minimum, put your dog in a sit and walk to the end of the lead. As you reach the end of the lead peep your whistle recall and give a little flick/gentle tug with your lead at the same time; keep walking, pat your left leg and say "heel". That reads as if it takes an awful lot of co-ordination, it doesn't really, just practice.

Do this little exercise on your walks as much as you can to teach your dog not only where the heel position is, but that it doesn't matter what you're doing, the heel position is always the same; by your left leg (unless of course you walk your dog on the right).

Once you're both comfortable with this little exercise put your dog, off lead, in a sit-wait and walk a smallish left hand circle around him, as you pass him whistle recall (or say "heel") and pat your left leg, he should get up and walk to heel with you. If he doesn't, then leave him on the lead and as you pass him pick it up and give him a wee flick.

Leave your dog in a sit-wait, then whistle recall him to heel...

...using your hand to guide him into position

Increase the distance between passing your dog on the circle and whistling him in to heel; also increase the distance between him catching you up and walking nicely to heel, to giving him lots of fuss so that he doesn't explode with excitement once he gets into the heel position.

Focus

The quickest and by far the easiest way to train your dog to focus his attention on you and seek eye contact is by using food, and I'm not talking about waving bits of chicken up by your eyes while you repeatedly say "watch me, watch me" in a high and grating way; we are gundog training after all.

Firstly, before we start, you'll need your lanyard in place and a handful of treats in your pocket. Stand in front of your dog with your dog in a sit and a treat in your hand. Put the treat right up to your dog's nose and before he gets a chance to eat it bring the same hand up to your lanyard, just above or on the whistle; your dog should follow your hand. As soon as your dog stops looking at your hand and looks at you give him the treat.

Over the next few sessions, as your dog looks at you, start talking to him, holding his gaze with yours and after a few seconds give him the treat. Build up the amount of time you're holding his gaze for – if he looks away stop talking immediately and return the treat to his nose to refocus him before continuing with the exercise.

The key with this bit of training is to keep your voice really dull, do not say your dog's name or even praise him - just very boringly talk at him. Over time you should be able to avert your gaze whilst still talking and your dog should keep looking up at you. Remember to do this exercise in the heel position once your dog has grasped the concept of looking at you when you give him the 'watch me' cue which is you taking hold of your lanyard.

Just imagine how cool it's going to be when you go on your first shoot and talk to the gamekeeper with your dog sitting beside you gazing up at you adoringly whilst you rest your thumb nonchalantly through your lanyard!

Training the Stand – A blonde moment, or should that be silver?

Talking about focus, I couldn't believe it when starting to plan my puppy book and realised that I'd missed how to teach your dog to stand within The Pet

Gundog. All I can do is put it down to a blonde moment, or as I'm more silver these days, a silver moment.

So here we have it, how to train your dog to stand, but before we do the how, first of all you need to know the why? Having a very pale Golden retriever the last thing I want to do is to put him in a sit-stay when it's very muddy whilst I cross stiles etc., also, when I hose my dogs down it's easier to put them in a stand stay, likewise when towelling them off. Good reasons for training the stand but the main reason though is for the vet; the stand for exam. The vet cannot get the thermometer where it needs to go if your dog is sitting or lying down, so, do your vet, yourself and your dog a favour and train a solid stand.

Have your dog sitting in the heel position on quite a short lead, a short lead not a tight lead; although the lead should be straight there shouldn't be any tension going through it. Hold your lead in your left hand and a sweetie in the right, then turn to face your dog and very slowly lure him forward with your right hand until he's standing. Use your lead to moderate the speed of forward movement and once he's on his feet say "stand" and allow him to nibble on the sweetie whilst you say "stand, good dog, stand".

You can also train this exercise from the down position, if you've taught it.

Quite simply put your dog into the down position. Put your treat on his nose and lure him into the standing position by moving the treat forwards and away from him whilst slowly lifting up at the same time. Don't lift the treat straight up as that will encourage him to go into the sitting position rather than the stand.

I find the best treats to use to train this exercise are things like shapes as you can hold on to them whilst your dog nibbles away in the standing position. Over time you will stroke and 'faff' with your dog whilst he's nibbling on the treat, for example massaging his ears, stroking his tail, lifting his paws and so on, so that he gets used to being touched whilst in the stand.

If your dog is inclined to sit or lie down as soon as he goes into the stand or if he tries to bottom shuffle, then as your dog moves into the stand position, slide your left foot along the ground so it's under his tummy, keeping your foot flat so you don't catch him with it as you do so.

Just imagine the shock you would have if you got up from a chair and went to sit back down again and something was on it – you'd pop straight back up; that is what sliding your foot underneath your dog's tummy without him realising it will do.

The basic retrieve
Training the basic retrieve was covered in depth in The Pet Gundog; as promised I'm not going to go over old ground (or at least I'm trying very hard not to), however I am going to use the summary of the sequence so that we can expand on it and to save you flipping between the two books.

And so to quote myself:

"The most important thing about teaching your dog to retrieve is that it's fun: fun for you and fun for your dog. It may seem as if there's a lot involved, well a lot more than just throwing a toy and letting your dog play fetch with it. There is. We're going for obedience and a way to channel the dog's mind from being scattered to having purpose; remember he has been bred to help you get your lunch and there's nothing that will bring more focus to a gundog than a retrieve.

So, he we go, the retrieve, from the top...

With your dog sitting to heel, tell him to wait and slide the foot closest to him back and throw the dummy, or the toy, so it lands more or less in front of him although at distance. As it lands say "mark". Tell him to wait again and stretch your arm out towards the dummy then look down at your dog to make sure he's looking in the right direction and cast him off with a 'Get On'.

When your dog has picked up the dummy praise him, whistle him back and smile. As your dog comes in pat your tummy (are you still smiling?) and tell your dog to sit in front of you. Take the dummy, tell him what a good boy he is and put him to heel, smiling as you do so.

Now break off from training and play with your dog!"

A lovely sit delivery is what we all aim for, however, if you're struggling achieving it without your dog spitting the dummy, then go for the next best thing which is a standing delivery followed immediately by your dog sitting in front of you.

As your dog comes in rather than give the sit command (verbally or with a hand signal), quite simply put one leg back, bend it and put your weight over it leaning back slightly, put your hand on the back bent leg. Once your dog has given you the dummy, stand up by bringing your back leg in while giving the hand signal for sit; this is to help your dog to come in really close with the delivery, as by having your weight back, you're inviting your dog into your space.

Once this is happening consistently you can then decide whether your dog comes in and delivers prior to sitting or after sitting, however, go for steadiness and always make your dog sit in front of you after the delivery until you say 'heel' – this is a great time to put your dummies away, blow your nose, rearrange your hat/scarf/bra-strap etc.

Remember you want the retrieve to be a pleasant experience for your dog; as we progress into the more advanced training the retrieve really is the reward and should be the 'be all and end all' to your dog, regardless of what breed your dog is, so,

- No snatching of the dummy when your dog brings it back; not only will it affect your delivery and make your dog start either spitting or hanging on to the dummy, you're communicating to your dog just how important the item in his mouth is.

- No reaching forward to take the dummy as the dog comes in; not only are you telling your dog how valuable the dummy is to you but you're also giving away how far you can reach and therefore how far away from you your dog needs to stop to be in control.

- No standing with your arms wide; you can do this initially to let your dog know where you are if for example you're wearing dark colours and standing against a dark background – the movement will help him to see you, however, if your arms are wide when your dog approaches you, all you are doing is causing confusion: should your dog put the dummy in your right hand or should your dog put the dummy in your left hand? You're also encouraging him to run out to the side rather than come in straight and front. Keep your hands in, either at your tummy, between your knees or resting on your bent back leg.

- No continuous calling (or whistling) of your dog when he is coming back with the dummy; if he's dicking about with it then it's time to go back to basics and get him back on the long line. When first training the retrieve, whistling or calling your dog back immediately is a great way of teaching your dog what is expected of him. Once he gets the hang of it you only need whistle him if you have more than one dummy down; again to teach him what's expected. After that he should know his job and should only need to be whistled if he's distracted or not coming back fast enough.

- No frowning at your dog when he's getting it right; smile, he'll come back quicker and with more enthusiasm if he thinks he's doing a good job and going to be rewarded for his efforts. If you're standing there frowning, which is what we are inclined to do when we are concentrating on getting something right, you're giving your dog mixed messages and making the learning process much harder than it needs to be.

Oh and finally, please don't allow your dog to have any dummies available at any time other than when he's working for you. I trained one dog who cast off beautifully and very enthusiastically then picked up the dummy and lay down to chew it like a chew stick; his favourite game according to his owner was to chew the end off a dummy, hold it by the toggle end and give it a good shake so all the sand came out - he would then tear the canvas into little pieces. "   !!!" was what went through my head.

Ready, Steady, Go

Steadiness is so important for any kind of dog regardless of whether that dog is from a gundog breed, or not, and whether he's going to work, or not. If you have a pet dog then you need to train him steadiness, not necessarily in the same way you would for a gundog, but steadiness should be high on the training agenda. Why? Well if you're walking your dog across a field and a rabbit runs in front of your dog, or in the woods a deer, or in the town a cat, or somewhere new coming across a field of sheep, then by training steadiness to moving objects there's a good chance your dog won't end up under a car or being shot by a farmer.

For gundogs however there is an added element in that at some point you're going to want them to take off after the object and so he needs to learn that until you say so, it's no go.

To train steadiness as part of the retrieve, simply train on a long line or a loose lead so that if your dog goes to run in, there is an instant consequence as the lead takes affect (if you can do this silently it will be more beneficial as it becomes a consequence of your dog's action that doesn't involve you). Every few retrieves make sure you go and pick up the dummy yourself, not just the short throws or short memory retrieves but the long ones too. Set yourself up to send your dog, including outstretching your arm towards the dummy and putting your weight over your front leg; at the last minute say 'stay' and walk out to collect the dummy yourself.

What is quickly becoming my favourite steadiness exercise at home is playing two balls. Once you've trained your sit-stay have your dog sitting between you and the wall but slightly off to the side, then throw one ball against the wall and catch it whilst keeping your dog in a sit. When your dog can remain seated then play two balls against the wall. When your dog can remain seated, kneel down so that the balls are passing in front of your dog's face, allow a ball to drop and so on. When I was a kid the game was 'Big Ben'... Big Ben strikes 10, Big Ben strikes 9, Big Ben strikes 8 and so on, for each number you had to do something different with the balls, for example bouncing them off the ground and catching them, throwing them in the air.

With my youngster the steadiness game I played with the balls, as well as Big Ben, was to throw and catch them in the air with him sitting at my side, every now and again I'd say 'catch' and he would jump up and catch one, holding it until I took it from him.

Angus was trying so hard not to look at the thrown dummy

Training steadiness can be great fun for both you and your dog and just takes a bit of imagination. When your dog is steady with tennis balls, up the ante and use rabbit skin covered balls, balls with treats inside, anything really.

Not everyone has access to a rabbit pen or a trainer that lives close by with one, however that doesn't mean you can't take your steadiness training to the next level. If you live near a river where there's ducks, take your dog to sit and watch you feed them. Just put him in a sit, give him a treat and throw a treat for the ducks, he'll learn very quickly that if he sits nicely while the ducks are quacking and squabbling and moving around he'll get a yummy reward.

Likewise if you're out walking and see a squirrel or two, don't avoid them, put your dog on lead and follow them while making your dog walk nicely to heel as you do so, and then stand and do nothing for a while.

After sitting nicely to heel while I fed the local ducks from around 5 months old, I decided to take my youngster down to a friend's rabbit pen when he was just under 10 months old. All the sitting and doing nothing at the river Kennet paid off and he just sat there watching the pheasants and rabbits running around whilst a spaniel did some retrieves; he was far more interested in sampling the various types of poo available!

Get in, get out, get up, get down, get off...

There are many different commands used in gundog training and generally the commands that you use will depend on the person you're training with or who set you on the path on gundog training.

I try to keep it as simple as possible so that trainers are consistent with their commands making it easier not just for their dog but for them also. I know of gundog trainers who have one command for a marked/seen, another for a blind, another for a runner and so on but for me that's a tad too complicated for the old grey matter and seriously too complicated for my Goldie.

There are only three commands that I insist that people use 'Get ON', Get OUT' and 'Go BACK', the rest is personal choice, however, if a handler has already trained different commands then rather than add confusion we leave well alone.

Get ON

All 'get on' means is to run in a straight line in the direction you are facing until you either find a retrieve or until I tell you to stop... simple huh?

This is the retrieve that we trained in The Pet Gundog and involves you lining your dog's pelvis up with the dummy, standing with both your feet pointing towards the dummy with your leg closest to your dog slightly further back, outstretching your arm towards the dummy and saying "get ON".

Your dog will be focused on the dummy when you send him and he'll run out in a straight line, collect the dummy and bring it back for lots of praise from you.

If you remember we trained this initially on a toy - by running in the direction you told him to, your dog would get the reward for doing as he was told, by bringing it back to you there was a reward of a different sort, this time praise and then more praise when you put him to heel.

Remember your dog, regardless of how much you want to think otherwise, is still an animal and follows the basic rule of survival 'what's in it for me?' As we extend your dog's training and introduce complexity please keep this question in your mind, it will make life a lot easier as a trainer and will help you understand why I train the way that I do.

Get OUT!

All 'get out' means is to turn 90° and run in a straight line in the direction that I'm pointing and looking until you either find a retrieve or until I tell you to stop. Slightly more complicated which is why before you train this command you need to have a solid and enthusiastic 'get on'.

As you might have guessed this is the start of directional control training, also known as lefts and rights and it is when you train your dog to follow the point.

I know when I start to do this I really feel as if I'm gundog training and not playing 'fetch' and the first time I trained it found the whole thing very exciting. Now as a behaviourist I still find the whole process of following the point fascinating; so much so that I did my Masters degree around it and am changing (or rather enhancing) the way that I train the command so what you're learning really is 'hot off the press', but more of that later!

Just so that you have the background, traditionally this exercise is trained against a fence line or on a track, however, I don't train it that way at all. In fact I don't train it on dummies or toys initially either... I use shape biscuits.

Most dogs will toilet along the fence line or hedge line and once one dog does other dogs follow – it becomes a massive communication centre with smells aplenty providing loads of distractions. On walks most dogs will head towards fence/hedge lines to investigate the contents therein – they're not daft; they know that that's where the bunnies run to. To train a new exercise under those conditions is setting a dog up to fail and this early in the training we should be aiming to set our dogs up to succeed every time.

Also at some point you're going to want to do this in the middle of a field and if your dog hasn't got the fence line to keep him straight going out then he can flounder.

When I first trained Bart, my black Labrador in The Pet Gundog, I decided to use his love of food to help me train direction control; that and the fact that we were renting a house at the time with a tiny garden and even smaller living room and I didn't want to hoist dummies round to the local park a couple of times a day to train him. And so without realising it, I developed a new way of training lefts and rights that is easy, stress free for the dog and loaded with rewards so that the dog gets it right first time and the owners get a warm and fuzzy watching their dog's progress through the complexity of gundog training.

Training Get OUT!

Before embarking on your lefts and rights please make sure you have a solid sit-wait otherwise you're going to find this challenging.

Pop a couple of shape biscuits in your pocket and your dog in a sit-wait. Leave him where he is and go and stand a couple of paces in front of him facing him, so that your knees are lined up with and facing his shoulders.

Give him the 'stop/wait/sit' hand signal (like a policeman's hand signal for STOP).

Walk in an arc from where you're standing around to his side, as if you're going to walk a smallish circle around him, then, when you get parallel to his shoulder repeat the wait command, show him the shape biscuit and put it on the ground.

It is really important that if your dog moves you say "no, wait", pick up the shape biscuit and continue on your circle until you can put the biscuit down parallel to his shoulder. You are now doing some serious steadiness training.

When you've got the shape biscuit on the ground with your dog sitting nicely, repeat your 'wait' command along with hand signal and then return to your starting position.

Once there repeat your 'wait' command and hand signal, keeping your hand out to steady your dog. Try to stand with your feet slightly apart.

I'm using a dummy here rather than shapes as shapes couldn't be seen clearly on the photo, however, start with the biscuits

Start leaning towards the shape biscuit and moving your hand slowly towards it; keep eye contact with your dog and repeat the 'wait' command.

When you are leaning slightly towards the side and have your arm out at 90° to your body, turn your head and look towards the biscuit, say "get out" and do a fast body movement towards it (as if you're pretending to go for it yourself), putting your weight very definitely over the foot closest to the biscuit.

Your dog will run to the biscuit and eat it. Once he's finished his reward call him to you with "come" and have him sit nicely in front of you – this is putting in the final behaviour of getting the reward and coming straight back.

If your dog is like my youngster he'll pick the biscuit up and come back to you before eating, that's fine let him do that and once he's finished his reward get him to sit nicely.

Repeat the above exercise two or three times in a row, two or three times a day to the same side only. This will not only cement the exercise in your dog's mind but will help with your co-ordination, making the exercise and movement part of your body's memory (a bit like learning to drive after a while, through masses of repetition, the process of driving becomes part of your body's memory and you can go on automatic pilot).

After a week start putting the biscuit down to the other side only. After a few days, as you give the 'wait' command (with hand signal) whilst standing in front of your dog prior to sending him, introduce the sit whistle; you'll be standing in front with your hand signal saying stop and you'll do a single pip.

In the real world you'll only ever do lefts and rights following on from the stop whistle so you might as well put the picture in your dog's brain now.

Introducing dummies

Once your dog can go out to the left or the right for a biscuit you can start using dummies. The set up is exactly the same except instead of putting down a shape biscuit you can put down a dummy. Please don't use an orange dummy to start off with as a dog can't see orange against green; these are for when you're challenging your dog, however they look so much better on photos than the green dummies do! (see 'Seeing is Believing', p48)

"Get OUT!"

Remember when you send your dog for the dummy to call him back so you get your nice delivery then either leave him sitting in front, step back and put your next dummy down or heel him back to the spot where you were training your exercise.

Keeping a relatively short distance between you and your dog and your dog and the dummy you can now start to put out two dummies. Put out one dummy in the manner that you have been, then return to the front of your dog, repeat the 'wait' command and put out the other, so your dog is sitting with a dummy to either side of him.

Return to the front of your dog and repeat the 'wait' command.

Take a sideways step towards the last dummy that you put down, repeat your 'wait' command, then, as you have been doing, send your dog for the last dummy.

The reason for sending your dog for the last dummy placed down is because that is the dummy that your dog will be more focussed upon; by taking a step towards it you're signalling your intention and making it easier for your dog to succeed.

When your dog is confidently bringing back the last dummy put down correctly, instead of taking a step towards it, just send him. You've got it, once he's confident doing that it's time to send him for the first dummy down; to make it easier for him take a sideways step towards the dummy signalling your intent and once he's retrieving that successfully then you can remain still.

If your dog is steady during this time you can start throwing the dummies instead of placing them down, however do it in graduated steps. Place a dummy down on one side, return to the front and throw a dummy to the other. When your dog looks at you send him for the thrown dummy. Again in time you can throw both dummies and as you both get proficient in the exercise can choose whether you send him for the first dummy down or the last.

When you and your dog are comfortable and confident doing lefts and rights it's time to start increasing the distances (see 'Upping the Ante', p46).

So what's changed then? or should I say enhanced?

The difference between what I've written and what you see in the photos for training the 'get out' is this; as you send your dog for the retrieve you 'turn your head and look towards the biscuit' or rather the 'thing' that you want your dog to retrieve.

At the end of March this year (2011) I carried out an experiment for my Masters degree on whether inherent behaviour or trained behaviour was more successful in getting a dog to go left or right; basically whether the dog followed 'the gaze' (inherent behaviour) in favour of 'the point' (trained behaviour).

You may have guessed that as I've incorporated 'the gaze' or rather 'the look' into my training of direction control, that inherent behaviour was very successful. I was so pleased with the photos that I'd had taken in January for this book that I didn't want to redo them and instead thought I would share the latest information with you and how it came about.

I cover my Masters degree in more detail at the end of the book.

Go BACK!

All 'go back' means is to turn 180° and run in a straight line until you either find a retrieve or until I tell you to stop. Slightly more complicated than the 'get out' and an exercise that shouldn't be trained until you have a solid and enthusiastic 'get out' otherwise I can more or less guarantee that confusion will reign.

The 'go back' was traditionally trained on a memory retrieve on a track and although it works, because I train 'go back to the left' or 'go back to the right' I want to make sure the dog understands the concept easily and so I train it in an open field.

Once your dog understands 'go back' then training it on a track is great, however, let's get both you and your dog really confident and comfortable with the exercise first.

Training Go BACK!

For this exercise I have always used a white dummy as I want to make sure my dog can see it as soon as he starts to turn, however you can now get blue and purple dummies which the dog can see even more clearly.

It's a good idea to start learning this with your non-dominant hand as, although it takes a bit more thought, if you start with your dominant hand you'll find it more difficult to make the transition across. I'll be describing it below as if you're right handed.

Pop your dog in a 'sit-wait', leave him where he is and go and stand a couple of paces in front of him facing him, as if you're getting ready to do your lefts and rights.

Give him the 'stop/wait/sit' hand signal and then walk three or four paces to your left (your dog's right) and then walk past your dog by a couple of paces.

Place a dummy on the ground so that it's a couple of feet behind but to the side of your dog.

Again, as with training the 'get out', any kind of movement from your dog and you repeat the 'wait' command and continue as you were until the dummy is placed as above.

Stand a couple of paces in front of your dog but to your left so that you're lined up with the dummy.

Raise your left hand to above shoulder level, palm facing your dog with your fingers together and 'push' the dog back with a 'go BACK'. Step forward as you do so to encourage the dog to move and look at the dummy... remember to smile or at the very least, try not to frown.

This is quite a tricky exercise to train and learn, so be patient, if your dog makes a mistake just set him up and try again.

When your dog understands what is required of him, then don't go as far to the left to give the hand signal, you're aiming to be standing in front of him as you give it. Once you can, it's time to do it to your right using your right hand to 'push' your dog back - just repeat the process as detailed above.

Although your dog will understand what is required quicker, it's important not to skip any of the stages as you want your dog to fully understand that when you use your left hand to 'push' him back he is to turn to his right and if you use your right hand to 'push' him back he is to turn to his left - basically he turns towards the hand raised.

When your dog is steady whilst placing down the dummies you can start to throw them; initially walk out to the side to throw as you did when you were placing them down as it will give your dog focus and make it easier to turn him. When he gets more advanced you should be able to stand in front of him and throw them over his head deciding only once they land whether you are going to send him back to the right or the left.

As with the lefts and rights, when standing in front of your dog prior to pushing him back, use your stop/sit whistle, however, use the hand that you're going to send him back with to give the hand signal... nothing looks more cack-handed than seeing someone use their right hand to stop their dog and then switch hands to send their dogs back, whereas it has got to be said that nothing looks cooler than to see someone stop and then smoothly send their dog back for a retrieve.

Mechanics of movement; looking after your dog

Both the 'get out' and the 'go back' cause huge amounts of strain on your dog's muscles, tendons and joints. Before you start to train them please make sure your dog has warmed up, either as part of your walk or by doing a couple of easy 'get on' retrieves first; don't go straight from dog snoozing at your feet to sitting up and training.

The photos of Angus doing the 'get out' shows just how fast he's turning on the spot; see the flattening of his cheek as the G-force takes effect. The amount of rotation that is taking place on his front legs and, in this instance, the left hip, is amazing – and that is just for a 90° turn on a 'get out'.

You see by the photos of Moss the strain on the joints as he twists 180° on the spot to do the 'go back'.

As he turns to his right he has to lean in, closing the angle of the elbow and putting tension on his wrist; his left tricep at this point is providing the power to spin him around and his left wrist is seriously over extended.

As he builds momentum his hind legs take the strain; as he twists his right leg under and pushes off, the angle is closed causing pressure at the hip

flexor, once he's out of the turn his left hind leg takes the strain on the inside as he pushes off and round.

The age for training either of these exercises should be taken into account also. A young dog that has loose joints and less than toned muscle tissue can get into all sorts of problems later on through over training these exercises.

I tend not to train 'get out' until the dog is seven or eight months old and the 'go back' until the dog is between eight and ten months. Not only do you have to do lots of repetition for both you and your dog to understand what is involved in the exercise and make it part of your tool kit, but once you start training it you'll be so excited by what you can do with your dog you won't be able to stop yourself.

Four dummies and a dog

I'm quite often asked what to purchase in order to progress with our gundog training and my response is always the same; a gundog, a lead, a whistle (preferably with a lanyard), four dummies and a couple of tennis balls.

I say four dummies but it doesn't have to be, four of anything will do; gloves, hats, scarves, toys and so on. And before you think I deliberately missed off infinite patience and a sense of humour, I didn't – I don't believe you can buy those in a shop.

For me though, you can't beat dummies, they're easy to carry, easy to wash, easy to find (most of the time) and providing you don't do girly throws near trees will last a very, very long time. Then when you want to add a bit of excitement, distraction or a bit of oomph to your retrieve get the fluffy, squeaky toys out.

There are a huge range of dummies available on the market now and I would recommend that you get a couple of each type if you can afford it, start with the plain 1lb ones, I prefer the softer mouth ones that Quest do (see useful contacts) as they're easier on the dog. Start with green and include a white one to teach your 'go back', an orange one never goes amiss either, unless of course you throw like a girl near a tree - believe me you think you'll only do this the once but you won't, you'll probably lose more dummies this way than any other, but I digress.

I would then increase your collection to include a partridge dummy and a pheasant dummy in either purple or black and white from the Working Dog Company (see useful contacts); these are great to help your dog hunt and to help him stretch his jaw as time goes on. A couple of rabbit skin covered tennis balls are fantastic for when you start training your dog to hunt in cover and a dokken or a foam pheasant always makes a wonderful addition to a Christmas or birthday list.

However, all of the exercises that follow can be done quite easily with the common garden variety 1lb softer mouth dummy.

Making it interesting

With four dummies in your training bag the world is your oyster, well more like the local park is your playground.

In The Pet Gundog I covered how to train the clock using the 'get on' command which involved putting down dummies at points on a clock face (just an imaginary circle really) and sending your dog for each dummy in turn. While this is a great exercise and one that you will continue to return to throughout your training, there are other exercises that you can train which, as well as being challenging, are also good fun.

The Split Retrieve

Also known as the Novice retrieve as it is quite often featured in Novice working tests and to train it you'll need two dummies.

Standing with your dog by your side, throw a dummy in front but to your left and another in front to your right; you're aiming for a 90° degree angle with you at the point of the V. Turn your dog so he's lined up with the last dummy thrown, the one on your right; when he locks on to it (you know that really intense look towards the dummy that tells you he's marked it) send him. Once he's presented nicely and sat in front for a second or two put him to heel and as you do so start turning to the left, moving your position so that when he arrives at the heel position he's lined up to the other dummy; when he's locked on, send him.

It's important when training one retrieve after another, that you get the first dummy out of the way, either tucked under your arm, attaching it via the toggle to a belt loop (if you're wearing jeans) or preferably popping it in a training bag or training vest (if you want to see what a training vest is I'm wearing one teaching the water retrieves later in this book); the last thing you want to do is to drop the dummy behind you or to the side as your dog will focus on that and you'll set him up to fail.

When you train multiple retrieves, especially when you start doing more complex work, remember that all you are doing is chaining together a couple of exercises. Look on each link as an exercise in its own right and complete the retrieve before sending your dog for the next one, for example making sure your dog sits in front for a second or so before popping him to heel – you're communicating to him that the 'fun' happens at your pace, not his and you'll have a steadier dog because of it.

Once your dog has mastered the basic split retrieve you can start to decrease the angle effectively reducing the distance between them. You can then, in time, choose which dummy your dog picks up.

Other ways that you can increase the complexity of this exercise are to send your dog for the first dummy thrown rather than the last and, so that your dog learns to extend his marking ability, leave your dog in a stay and walk out a couple of paces before you throw your dummies. It means that you no longer work with the letter V in mind but rather the letter Y; with your dog left in a stay, walk to the fork and throw your dummies and then return to your dog to send him, thereby increasing the distance of the retrieve.

The Segment

The segment is really just half a clock with a dummy placed at 9, 12 and 3 or 3, 6 and 9, however, now that you have lefts and rights within your toolkit you can take it to another level.

Pop your dog in a sit facing you. Throw a dummy over his head to the 12 o'clock position, then one to your right (3 o'clock) and one to your left (9 o'clock). As in the way of teaching something new, send your dog for the 9 o'clock dummy with a 'get out' as that was the last dummy thrown.

As you put your dog to heel move your position so that by the time your dog gets to your left leg he's lined up with a dummy and, when he's settled, send him with a 'get on'.

Repeat it so that the last dummy down varies between 3 and 9, forget about the dummy behind your dog initially and look on it as a distraction dummy.

When you're both really confident with using the segment this way you can start to introduce the 'go back'. Leave your dog in a sit and place (don't throw initially) a dummy to either side of him. Stand in front and throw a dummy over his head and when he looks to you again, send him with a 'go back' either to the left or the right depending on which side the dummy landed on.

When your dog gets the hang of this then place a dummy to his side, quietly throw a dummy to the other side and noisily throw one behind him using the brruuuppp bbrrruuuuppp noise to focus his attention on the last dummy down, as soon as he looks back to you send him.

Remember if your dog gets it wrong not to get wound up, you're doing some very complicated training; go back a couple of stages and try not to rush things - check your body language and facial expression, take some of the pressure off and have a bit of fun.

Always end on a high note, even if you feel you've gone back a step. Learning takes time: two years, on average, to train a gundog; ten minutes to break one.

The Advanced Clock

By the time you get to work the advanced clock you will have grown to love using the clock for your training; whenever I'm short on time I use the clock as it's a quick way to do some training and tire out a gundog in a short space of time and as everyone knows a tired dog is happy dog, or rather a dog not looking for mischief.

Initially put down four dummies in any way you like, whether that's walking around the outside and dropping them (with or without your dog), walking a cross, standing beside your dog and throwing them out or throwing them over your dog's head; I think that covers all the ways of putting them down.

To make it easier to explain and follow I'll make it precise; as you get used to using many commands one after the other then play around with it, but for now:

- Start by standing in the middle of the clock and have your dog to heel facing the 12 o'clock position; send him for the dummy with a 'get on'. Leave him sitting in front of you and take a step back.

- Send him for the 3 o'clock dummy with a 'get out' (to the right). Step back into the centre and turn to face him (3 o'clock) as he comes back and put him to heel following delivery. Leave him there, take a couple of steps away from him so you're walking towards 3 o'clock and turn to face him.

- Send him for the 9 o'clock dummy with a 'go back'. Leave him sitting in front of you and take a step back.

- Send him for the 6 o'clock dummy with a 'get out' (to the left).

- I always say to my handlers, especially when doing the advanced clock, not to rush things, take your time, take a breath and pause whilst your dog is sitting nicely in front of you to think about what you're doing next; no one watching will ever know that you're trying to figure out what to do next and gathering your thoughts; they'll think you're just doing some steadiness training.

- When you're comfortable using the advanced clock start putting dummies down at 12 o'clock, 2 o'clock, 4 o'clock and 6 o'clock and when you're happy working with the dummies closer together invest in another two and put them down at 8 o'clock and 10 o'clock as well.

Upping the Ante

Whenever you increase the complexity of an exercise you need to decrease either the distance or the duration; likewise if you increase the duration or distance of an exercise you need to decrease the complexity.

Using the 'go back' exercise as an example; to start off with you only have five or six feet between you and your dog and five or six feet between your dog and the dummy. As you stretch your dog's ability you may put the dummy ten feet or so behind your dog keeping five feet between you. You then have a choice of leaving the dummy at ten feet and moving back ten feet or moving the dummy back to fifteen feet - you wouldn't move both yourself and the dummy back at the same time.

Try to think of it like a bead on a string with a knot at each end; the dog being the bead and one of the knots being your dummy and the other knot being your good self. As you move the bead away from one knot it gets closer to the other. Similarly as you move your dog further away from the dummy your dog is positioned closer to you, likewise if you move your dog further away from you he gets closer to the dummy.

Remember, adding a distraction in training will automatically take the exercise up another level. We did lots of distraction training in The Pet Gundog in relation to stays but haven't as yet introduced any to the retrieve. When your dog is retrieving enthusiastically and flying back to you with the dummy start throwing a dummy out whilst he's on the move. So, you send your dog for an easy retrieve and as he returns throw a dummy out to the side and insist he comes in with a nice present. Send him for the dummy you've just thrown and when he comes back throw the previously retrieved dummy off to the other side.

When he can keep his concentration on coming in with a nice delivery whilst you throw a dummy out to the side, start to throw it over his head instead, you can then choose whether you're going to put him to heel following the first retrieve and send him for a simple 'get on' or whether you're going to take a step back and send him with a 'go back'.

Another way to increase the complexity of your 'go back' and keep it interesting was told to me by a lady called Wendy Neville who has attended a couple of training days with me. Find a fork in a track and sit your dog slightly forward of it; put a dummy down each track and either send your dog down the right track or left depending on which hand you use.

Likewise if you came to a T in a track you could enhance your 'get out' training. Put your dog slightly up the 'I' with a dummy at either end of the bar, whistling your dog off the mark so that he comes forward slightly then give him the hand signal and 'get out' command.

Please be aware that when you up the ante it's easy to fall into the trap of pushing your dog too hard. We tend to get quite engrossed in new things, but our dogs can get burnt out, bored, or stressed with the new, more complicated training. Several short training sessions, each ending with an easy retrieve are the order of the day.

Extend your dog's abilities; give him something familiar to end on and you'll both finish your session on a high.

Seeing is believing... Not in the dog's world

You know the saying "seeing is believing"? Well that isn't necessarily so for the dog at your feet. We humans put an awful lot of faith in what we see and many of our sayings stem from it "seeing is believing", "do my eyes deceive me", "have your eyes wide open", "do you see what I mean" and for the visual learners "do you see what I'm saying".

One of the things that I'm seeing more and more of at the training days that I run are handlers sprawling over their dog's back, getting as low and in the dog's personal space as possible whilst casting them off. Called 'align the spine' it's to try and get yourself as close to your dog's perspective as you can, so that you can see what your dog sees. I believe I have, on more than one occasion, said it was absolute nonsense.

I can only presume that the principle behind it is like trying to line up a snooker cue on the white ball, the difference being that you rest your chin on the cue and lower yourself so that you can see straight down the cue to where it hits the white ball and 'see' the line that not only your cue ball is going to take but also your marked ball.

Well it doesn't work like that with casting off dogs. Even if you straddle your dog like he's a pony and put your chin up against the base of his skull and look across the top of his forehead (after keeping his head clamped still that is) you'll not see what he sees, and that's even whilst presuming your eyes are pointing in the same direction as his.

Why not? Well, partly because of his amazing sense of smell, but mainly because the anatomy and physiology of our sense of sight is different.

In both humans and canines the retina of the eye is lined with photoreceptor cells which respond to light and, using electrical impulses, sends messages via the optic nerve to the brain. There are two types of photoreceptor cells; rods and cones. Rods are motion detectors and process visual information in dim or poor light whereas cones process colour and detail and work best in medium to high levels of light.

Rods are prevalent in both species, more so in the dog than us, however the same can't be said for cones. The central retina in the dog's eye contains approximately 20% cones whereas we have an area of 100% cones called the fovea.

Humans and canines evolved differently, including their senses. We tended to hunt during the day (diurnal) so night vision wasn't hugely important to us, however our ability to determine different colours to help us forage for food and 'see' what is ripe and what is not is important.

Wolves are not diurnal and neither were the early types of dogs, it's only been part of the domestication process that makes them so; wild dogs still hunt at night. The ability to see in the dark therefore, outweighs the need to see vibrant colour and, let's face it, most of the dog's prey is camouflaged; they tend to rely on their ability to detect movement along with their heightened sense of smell to survive.

Do you remember at school, probably in art being taught about the three primary colours? Red, blue and yellow; all of the colours that we see are a combination of the three. That is because we have three different types of cones; we're classed as a 'trichomat' species whereas the dog only has two different types of cones and is classed as a 'dichromat' species.

Putting it simply (sorry, it's all gone a bit technical) dogs are colour blind; not seeing in black and white only, as used to be thought, but are blind to certain colours. Using the colour spectrum you can 'see' why orange dummies are more difficult for a dog to work with than olive green, purple and blue. If you were to place an orange dummy on the grass both would appear to be 'yellow' to the dog and it's only his sense of smell that directs him to it; if however he had marked the dummy's fall then it would be the motion that drew him into the area ready for his nose to take over.

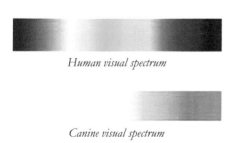

Human visual spectrum

Canine visual spectrum

We will never be able to see what our dog sees; the best we can do is point him in the right direction, hope he runs straight and then follows his nose. So give him a break and give him some space to be able to use his senses to the max rather than clog them with freshly applied deodorants, perfumes, aftershaves and a million other smells that that we force onto our dog as we drape ourselves over him to cast him off.

The Nose knows

The sense of smell is the one, certainly in humans and no doubt in dogs too, that evokes the most memories. Think of getting a waft of some freshly baked bread, immediately you think of how it tastes or it may take you back to when you were a child and your Mam was baking, or maybe standing in line at the local bakers shop with your mates from school.

The sense of smell is very different from the other special senses as it is the only one that spans time. Think about the amount of times you've walked into a room and known, for example, that someone has been smoking in there or been eating a bacon sandwich, or what about when you walk into your bedroom five minutes after your partner has just put their hairspray or deodorant on; the smell is there, it lingers, hanging in the air - images and sounds don't.

The dog's sense of smell and our sense of smell are similar but different. We both have nostrils (although the dogs are mobile and they can tune individual nostrils towards a smell that interests them), and the lining of our noses creates mucus which dissolves the odour molecules allowing the olfactory receptors (scent receptors) to send the information to our brain. That and apart from the fact that we have a measly 5 million scent receptors in our nose whereas our dogs have a whopping 220 million, is kind of where the similarity ends.

Unlike our nasal cavity, the dog's nasal cavity is hairless and has microvillus on the surface instead; they also have two extra 'pieces of equipment' in their skulls.

The vomeronasal organ, also called Jacobson's organ (at the time of writing it was still under debate whether this exists in adult humans and if it does, if it provides extra benefit to the sense of smell or communication), is an additional olfactory chamber lined with scent receptors which are different to the scent receptors in the nose. It is located behind the upper incisors just above the roof of the mouth and consists of two fluid-filled sacs which open into either the mouth or the nose. It is Jacobson's organ that is believed to be important in the deciphering of body scents accounting for the dog's ability to recognise other animals, as well as the change in hormones and pheromones (you know... the smell of fear).

The second piece of equipment that we don't have and which I personally find really fascinating is 'The Shelf' or to give it its proper name 'the subethmoidal shelf' which is a bony 'pocket' found below the bones of the nasal cavity. When a dog sniffs, which is an interruption of normal breathing, the air is forced into the shelf where the odour molecules are trapped. When the dog exhales, the molecules remain behind and accumulate; the shelf is never washed out which is why a dog can recognise a scent and follow a trail.

There have been many tests and experiments in relation to the dog's nose, but the one that makes me go 'wow!' was the one run by the US Army in the mid-eighties. It had already been established that a dog could track a person wearing rubber boots and then jumping on a bike; it is believed that the dog will pick up a combination of scents, for example person, boots, bike tyre rubber and broken grass stems, The Army however, took it to the next level.

They laid a track across a field and had the trackers use scuba equipment to swim underwater before emerging downstream and leaving on the opposite bank. They then deeply ploughed the field, covered it in petrol and set it alight and sprinkled it with spent and live ammunition - you know how this ends don't you? Yup, the dog's nose, and the dog of course, found the trackers.

Find it!

In The Pet Gundog we taught our dogs to sniff on command using 'find it' and digestive biscuits. It really is the easiest way to train a dog to get his head down and hunt for a scent, so regardless of where you are, you should be able to give your dog his 'find it' command and he should lower his head; if he doesn't you need to go back and train it in preparation for what comes next.

The nose really does know you know...

How much does your dog smell you and how much do you smell your dog?

I know that my dogs smell me a lot, especially after I've been working other people's dogs; they read my left leg like the daily newspaper... that is until I tell them enough. I don't mind them having a glancing read but when they want to settle down as if I'm a Jilly Cooper novel then I draw the line, however, I didn't realise just how much attention they paid to it. I normally wear an Estee Lauder perfume, Beautiful, and one of my closest friends wears a Clinique perfume, Happy. One day I decided to try it on, when I got home and Angus smelled my wrist he did a double take at my face; it was so funny, you could almost see him processing 'but you're Lez how do you smell of Jill!'

Have you ever smelled your dog? I encourage all my handlers to smell their dogs so that they know what they smell like when they're healthy, then, if their dog ever gets poorly, they (and now you) will be able to smell the difference.

And they love being smelled you know, they think it's great that you're down and doing 'dog stuff', especially if you do the sniffing thing in trains of sniffs rather than just breathing in their smell; they get all excited and, if you're on all fours, will try to get underneath you.

If you have more than one dog you'll be amazed at how differently they smell. I can still remember how Bart smelled when he was a puppy and how it changed as he matured; the bizarre thing was, when he died he smelled like he was a puppy again.

Blind retrieves; it's a trust thing

In The Pet Gundog we touched on blind retrieves and how to train them around the home and have some fun with your dog, now however, we start doing some grown up stuff.

Blind retrieves are, as you might guess, about your dog retrieving blind - that doesn't mean blindfolded it means that your dog doesn't see the dummy going down and he has to trust your judgement that there is something there for him to go and get for you.

The training that you're doing with your dog now really is very advanced and I'd be surprised if you haven't already had an audience whilst out in the local park doing some training. When I run sessions in public areas or are out training with some mates, the amount of people that stand and watch is quite amazing really; and they're normally not even gundog enthusiasts. It must be a very primordial thing to watch one species do the bidding of another; to watch man and dog hunting together, even if it is just for bags of sand.

Blind but seen... seen but blind...

Remember the memory or the dropped retrieve that we did way back when in The Pet Gundog? Good, it's the memory retrieve that you're going to be using to train your dog to do blind work. Find yourself a track on your usual walk, preferably one that has a long straight stretch and then bends or curves slightly. Walk down the track with your dog to heel, drop the dummy, about turn and walk twenty or so paces before about turning again to face the dummy; you should be able to see it. When your dog has locked on to the dummy, send him for the retrieve.

When he's comfortable doing this start dropping it as you walk down the track, without about turning and retracing your steps; just drop the dummy and keep walking a dozen or so paces, then about turn and send your dog when he's locked on.

Slowly increase the distance of the retrieve and start placing the dummy around the bend; if there are any fallen logs on the track even better.

To start your blind work away from a beaten track you repeat the process but start with shorter distances. Find a tree, a bush or a fence post to put a dummy at the bottom of, let your dog mark it and heel him ten to fifteen paces away; about turn and send him when he's locked on to the position. Always return to the same point for sending your dog from, so that there's a familiarity to the surrounding area for him. After a little while leave your dog in a sit and place the dummy out, returning to your dog to send him.

In time, either increase the distance or change where you send your dog from but don't do both at the same time. Remember another way to increase the complexity of any retrieve is to put down orange dummies; your dog won't see them and you may have to use your 'find it' command to help him out when he's in the right area which is why it's important to teach 'find it' prior to starting your blind work and hunting.

If you take your time with this and set your dog up to succeed every time, it won't take you too long before you can point your dog to a marker in the distance and say "get on" and your dog will cast off for you; it really is a trust thing.

Once you start to work off the beaten track, away from prominent markers, or you start training in a forest you may want to invest in some really colourful cord or ribbon so that you can tie it to the tree, or the bush, that you've put your dummy near, as once you walk away from the mark you'll lose sight of it. You wouldn't believe (or maybe you would) the amount of times I've put dummies down for my handlers, returned to them to say which tree the dummy is behind and had to turn around and walk straight back out again to check where they were as all the trees looked alike and I've gotten confused!

Working in cover... The Hunt

Teaching a dog to hunt and use his nose whilst in cover shouldn't be breed specific; although, it has got to be said, the spaniels and hunting groups do have the edge over the retrievers.

Before getting your dog to hunt in cover, first you have to teach your dog to hunt on command. It comes quite naturally to the majority of gundogs and they'll be back and forwards in their noses on walks, hunting and tracking under their own steam, however, we don't want them doing it for themselves – we want them doing it for us!

When you're out with your dog in the morning and he has some free time to get into his nose, watch how he moves; depending on his breed will depend on how he hunts. Spaniels for example, tend to be nose glued to the ground with ears falling either side of their noses providing the perfect funnel for those scent molecules to be drawn up into the shelf, their tails will be going twenty to the dozen, more so when they find the retrieve; Labradors too tend to run with their noses low but tend to do more of a sweeping movement rather than the fast, busy turning of the spaniel; Goldies, like flatcoats, will air scent, running along with their heads in the air then turning and running back again at the last minute dropping their noses for the retrieve.

All dogs have their own individual hunting style although the 'stamp' of the group that they belong in will be present. When Bart my old lab got on a scent he would transform from pet to predator, you could see the intensity of the hunt on his face and he'd be head down, tail up and going for it... until he got almost to the retrieve (whether that was a rabbit ball, a dummy or a bird) then his tail would drop and start wagging with all the emotion and surge in adrenaline.

When Angus my Goldie hunts he looks like such a poseur; no really he does. He's all blonde and flouncy while he's air scenting and does this little flick with his head as he turns back on the line to pick up the scent again – I keep saying I should get him on a Pantene advert! Once he's in the area then the look of concentration on his face is wonderful to behold, he turns from flouncy floozy to ferocious hunter in a second (well not quite ferocious but you get the idea), then it's head down and straight back up with a dummy or a bird. When we're out shooting we're often told "can you and Angus just go flounce over there".

Ziggy my youngster is heading in the same direction as Bart, his uncle, if not more so; he's certainly more intense, more focussed and at eleven months old, a lot steadier.

There will be times when the natural hunting pattern changes; if you haven't already been keeping a training diary then I suggest you start one and include observations from your walks, especially your early morning ones and you'll see the pattern for yourself - it's to do with ground temperature and whether there is any wind.

Smells are just tiny chemical molecules that float through the air that can get inhaled into our nasal cavities, and in the dog's case, into his shelf so it makes sense that the shift in scent, and therefore scent tracking, will be affected by the weather and ground temperature. An easy way to understand or think about how scent moves is to watch cigarette smoke; not after someone's inhaled it but what it does when the lighted cigarette is 'resting'. Sometimes it will swirl and curl, other times it will dissipate; likewise with morning mist. Not only is this affected by the movement of the wind but as the ground temperature warms up the mist rises – watch your dog in early morning mists, he'll either be trying to get his nose under the mist line (which consists of water droplets) or will be keeping it above it.

When you get more advanced with your training you'll take into account the direction of the wind, sending your dog downwind of the retrieve so that he can pick up the scent easier and use his nose to get him into the area. To work out which way the wind is blowing, pick a couple of blades of grass and hold them at 'dog height' and then just let them go; by dropping them at dog height rather than human height will indicate what is going on at your dog's level, which may be very different to the swaying trees and bushes in the distance.

Back and forwards, forwards and back

We've already trained our dogs to drop their noses when in an area to hunt on command, but what about teaching them or rather enhancing the pattern they take when hunting and getting them to hunt in front of you. This is generally known as 'quartering', or 'holding a pattern', although I tend just to refer to it as hunting.

If you have a spaniel then you'll be well aware of this movement as it comes so naturally to them; the key though is to keep the spaniel working close to you and not a million miles away which is often the case when out walking.

Why close? Well, a spaniel's job is to flush up game just in front of you so that you can shoot it. If your dog is working too far away, when the bird is flushed it's out of shooting range and you'll miss your lunch and go hungry for the day.

I always start to train this exercise in grass that is ankle length if possible, just enough to cover a tennis ball. Have a tennis ball in your left pocket and your dog walking to heel before you start the 'quartering game'. Using your right hand draw your dog away from your leg, clicking your fingers and saying "he, he, he" (as in here, here, here... the choice of words are yours, as is the clicking but many gundog folk use "he, he, he") and point to the grass; when he gets there repeat to the left, moving away from the direction your were taking; when he gets there and has a snuffle do the same to the right and quietly take the ball out of your pocket and drop it slightly behind you; as you do the "he, he, he" to the left point him towards the tennis ball, when he finds it and brings it to you give him masses of praise. Keep it fun and keep it light hearted.

Always help your dog when first starting to hunt in cover

It is entirely up you how you send your dog hunting... I tend to say "where is it?" (as opposed to 'weeezit') and once my dog is ahead will click my fingers and say "he, he, he" and when my dog turns, use my outstretched arm but pointing down and out (rather than just out as I would when sending for a 'get out') to help him move in the direction that I want him to. Others I know use 'seek it out', 'go on then' as well as a combination of commands.

Regardless of whether you plan to go shooting with your spaniel or not, this is a fantastic thing to train; you have your dog hunting on your behest rather than on his own, he's looking to you to see what you want him to do next, he's close to you which means he's safe from harm and, as an added benefit, you'll wear him out and as you know a tired dog is a happy dog and more importantly a dog that's not looking for mischief... music to the pet gundog owner's ears.

If you find that your dog is starting to creep too far away from you when training this exercise, or when out walking or working, go back to basics and put him on a long-line until he gets used to hunting close, then, as for training the recall, allow him to drag it behind him for a couple of weeks so that you can stand on it if need be.

When you get further on in the book you'll be able to combine your hunting exercise with the turn on the whistle, but for now, click your fingers or say "he, he, he" to get your dog working for you.

One of the things you do need to be aware of when you train your dog to hunt is to keep your non-working hand out of the way as it will cause confusion if you're waving both of your arms around; in the same way as when you trained direction control, keep your hand signals clear.

Whet your whistle

Before you can consider any kind of control at a distance you have to aim for 100% control by your side. The further your dog gets away from you the less control you will have. This is why we spend such a lot of time training various exercises on lead and close to you, for example whistle sitting to heel and recall to heel on the move, hoping that when you put some distance between yourself and your dog the commands still work.

When you start working your dog at distance really is when you start to appreciate whistle training; the last thing you want is to be standing in the middle of the field hollering like a fishwife at your dog to 'sit' or 'come'. Saying that, there is nothing more irritating than hearing someone constantly blowing the whistle.

I was attending a game fair a couple of years ago and stopped to watch one of the scurry events. The lady on the outside of the ring was offering the young handlers 'advice' and that advice was that as soon as the dog got the dummy to whistle, whistle, whistle, whistle, whistle not only constantly but loudly, so maybe I should have written WHISTLE, WHISTLE, WHISTLE, WHISTLE.

We walked away in disgust, another really nice dog and potential handler of the future ruined.

Sit

If you have the kind of dog that gets up in a stay when you approach him or one that shuffles forwards once you've stopped him on the whistle then you need to do some work with your dog tied up. Tying up whilst training can be so useful, not only does it give you an extra pair of hands but it makes your dog realise you don't have to be beside him for commands to be enforced.

Find a fence or a post (the old fashioned washing line posts are perfect) and make sure your dog is wearing a flat collar as opposed to a slip. Then tie him up, not too short, the lead should be loose but not long either – you don't want your dog to be able to move forward towards you. Whistle sit, give your stay command (if you use both, otherwise just the sit whistle and hand signal will suffice) and leave your dog. In your own time return to your dog; if he goes to get up stop moving, give the sit hand signal along with either the verbal or whistle command. As soon as your dog sits back down start moving towards him again. It may be a long drawn out process for you but it is very effective in teaching your dog that the only way he can get close to you, which is what he wants if he's on the move towards you, is to sit nicely until you return. Remember not to stroke him unless he is sitting.

Stop

Here follows some really effective ways of getting snappy whistle sits/stop at distance, some you will be ready to try now and others you'll have to wait until you've done more retrieving ('get out' for example), however, I thought I'd put them all in one place so you know where to find them when you're ready.

Whistle sit for dinner

Give the whistle sit command and as soon as your dog sits, either release him to start his dinner or put his dinner down for him to have.

Using a thrower; heeling away

Have a friend throw a dummy for you so that lands it more or less at their feet but slightly to the side of them; heel your dog away and as you do so have your friend quickly and quietly pick up the dummy and hide it behind their back.

Send your dog to where the dummy had landed and as soon as the dog looks unsure or puts his head down to start hunting blow your sit whistle. Your dog will be feeling unsure of himself and will respond better to help at this moment rather than when he's feeling confident. Once your dog is sitting nicely, praise him quietly at distance and have your thrower quietly drop the dummy behind them. As they move away direct your dog to the dummy.

Congratulations, your dog has just learned that you know best - when he was floundering around looking for the dummy, you stepped in and took control; as soon as he took direction from you the dummy miraculously appeared.

Step in to your dog on a recall

Leave your dog in a wait, and when you're ready, call him to you. After he's moved 4-5 strides do an elongated sit whistle along with the hand signal and step in towards your dog. Keep walking towards him until he puts his backside on the ground, then back off a couple of paces and smile to indicate your approval. Go up to your dog and quietly praise whilst his backside is still on the ground, give him a sweetie if you feel inclined – I usually do, especially early on in the training then go back to where you were and finish off your recall.

Out of all of the ways to train a whistle stop **this is the most efficient** but it can also unnerve some dogs and make others sticky on the recall. You can also do this around the house when your dog is mooching or sniffing at things; just walk at him and use your whistle and hand signal, as above, and as soon as he sits, back off, smile and then either walk over to him and give him a fuss or call him to you for one.

If you are going to train the stop this way, then make sure for every stop that you do, you do four or five unpressured recalls in between.

Using a thrower to step in

Have a friend throw a dummy for you so that when the dummy lands it's on the other side of them and slightly off to the side – so that they're standing between you and the dummy but you still have a straight run to it. Send your dog and whistle stop before he gets to your friend. As you whistle, your friend should step in front of the dummy (thinking "mine!" as they do so). Once your dog has stopped, walk out and calmly praise him then return to your original position and, once your friend has moved out of the way, send your dog for the retrieve. Don't use this technique if your dog is a little bit sticky when being sent for a retrieve or is wary or lacking confidence around people.

Training on your own

Leave your dog in a sit, walk about 8-10 paces and then throw a dummy so you're between the dummy and your dog but off to the side. Send your dog for the dummy and as your dog starts getting close to you peep on your whistle and step in front of the dummy (thinking "mine!") whilst at the same time giving a very definite hand signal. Once your dog is sitting, calmly walk out to him with a big smile on your face, give him praise (and a sweetie) and return to your original position. Send him for the retrieve with a smile on your face so that he knows it is okay to get up and give him lots of praise on the delivery. Again this is challenging for the less than bold dog so please don't use it if your dog is lacking confidence or is sticky when being sent for a retrieve.

My absolute favourite; using a toy

Last but by no means least, my favourite way of training a whistle sit whilst my dog is out in front is using a toy. Have a tennis ball or small toy in your hand and 'tease' your dog with it, encouraging him to play and chase the toy without actually getting it. Pretend to throw the toy just in front of you so that your dog moves slightly away from you, as he turns towards you, raise the hand that has the toy in it and blow your sit whistle - the second your dog sits throw the toy directly towards their mouth (although at this point he'll still be quite close to you, so dropping the toy in his mouth would probably be a more accurate description).

You need to keep your arm up in the air and throw the toy from that position rather than bringing it down by your side to throw it as you want your dog to raise its head to look at your hand. Remember that the mechanics of movement is that when your dog's head comes up his backside goes down, however, just in case it doesn't, when he looks up after your sit whistle say "sit".

Allow your dog to play with the toy for a couple of moments and then call him in, take the toy and repeat the game. Dogs love this game and, once you've trained a really solid 'get on' you'll be able to send your dog out, and blow the sit whistle after a couple of strides, when your dog sits, lob the toy towards his mouth. As always, once your dog is comfortable with the concept of sitting away from you, build up the time and distance between whistling and releasing the toy.

Turn

In some ways it's easier to turn your dog on the whistle rather than stop your dog on the whistle. Why? Well by the time you get to this stage in your training you should have an excellent recall and the 'turn' whistle is, in effect, the beginning of your recall.

I've used it many times in training and in demonstrations but only once for real on a shoot. A few years ago I sent my Labrador for a bird without realising it was in the area of a peg dog that I hadn't seen, making the retrieve his rather than mine; my Shoot Captain let me know and I quite simply double-peeped, Bart turned to look and I gave him a 'get out' signal to my right to draw him away from the bird. It worked; he turned away from the shot bird and started to hunt in the area I directed him to. I have to say, I was really rather pleased with my boy as it would have looked absolutely terrible if he'd ignored me.

My recall whistle is peep-peep, peep-peep; the first double peep will turn my dog and the second double peep will bring him to my heel. If your recall whistle is peep-peep-peep then you would use the first two peeps as your turn command. It really is quite easy to train and looks very cool when you and your dog have mastered it.

To start off with you can teach it on your own but you will, before long, need a friend to help.

Take a dummy with you on your usual walk and when your dog is a little way ahead, do a double peep on your whistle; as your dog turns throw your dummy to the side and give your 'get out' command.

Your dog has turned to face you and got an instant reward in the form of a retrieve. Have him deliver nicely, praise him and send him on his way so you can play the 'turn on the whistle' game again.

You can also throw the dummy in the opposite direction to your dog so that he has to run past you in order to get the retrieve; in this instance it would be the 'get on' command that you would use as your dog is facing the direction that you're sending him.

Once you've got to grips with turning and sending your dog on, then enlist the help of friend. You both need a dummy for this one. Have your thrower drop a dummy for you so that it lands to the side and slightly behind them, send your dog as usual and when he gets around 10 to

15 away from the dummy (or from your friend) double peep.

If he doesn't turn immediately your friend should quietly step in front of the dummy preventing the retrieve from taking place should your dog ignore you. As soon as your dog turns towards you, throw out your dummy and send your dog for his reward.

When he's turning without your friend having to cover the dummy you can do the exercise on your own.

Remember not to over train the exercise though as you don't want your dog to start pre-empting being turned off a dummy and becoming sticky; maybe only do this one in every ten retrieves.

They're, Their...THERE!

Actually it's just 'there' but couldn't resist taking you back to your school days – do they still teach that or am I showing my age?

The last whistle command that I use, and train, is the hunting whistle. Once I've established, well established that is, the head down and use your nose on the 'find it' command, then I start to add the whistle. Before you use it you need to decide what your hunting whistle is going to sound like and practice it. It needs to be distinct from your recall and sit whistles, as well as any other whistle commands that you use, it should also be a quiet whistle: if your dog is hunting something, especially in company, the last thing you want to do is blast repeatedly on the whistle. No, a quiet 'discreet' whistle is best if you don't want to irritate your fellow gundoggers – and I have to say it, some of the hunting whistles I've heard I've wanted to... well I'll leave it to you to fill in the blanks, but you get the idea don't you.

When I've demonstrated my hunting whistle verbally, that is off the whistle, I've been told it sounds like a pigeon; tu toooo tu toooooo. I tend to do it in blocks of two so it would be tu toooo tu toooooo pause tu toooo tu tooooooo

Harry getting his nose down and hunting on command

to give my dog a chance to use his nose and find the retrieve; if he's still in the hunting area and hasn't found anything I'll repeat the command, however, I don't constantly blow the hunting whistle or rely on it to tell my dog what to do. If I send him for a retrieve and he looks as if he's going to run straight over the dummy then I'll use it, or, if he's struggling to find the dummy, for whatever reason, then I'll help him out otherwise I tend to trust his nose and give him a chance to use it.

Harry following his nose

So how do we train it? When your dog is hunting, intersperse your 'find it' command with your hunting whistle - that's it really. If you use the whistle straight away you risk your dog misinterpreting the whistle for a recall so when your dog first puts his nose down say "find it", then use the hunting whistle, then "find it" again. It won't take long for your dog to put the action on the whistle, especially if you have a really well trained 'find it' command.

Accessorising!

... and I don't mean purchasing dummy vests to match your latest jacket and boots – oh okay, maybe I do.

Many times I've caught the guys who train with me roll their eyes when us girlies start talking about the latest training vest, boots and furry wellie liners, although they're so used to it now that they tend to join in. But no, I mean accessorising your training kit. We tend to start with a training bag and some green canvas dummies, then we may add an orange one or two and a couple of different shaped dummies; then it's rubber/plastic dummies and rabbit skin balls, as well as maybe a training vest for us. There comes a time though when you need to start thinking about preparing your dog to pick up game and that is when you start to accessorise what you already have.

Dressing your dummy
The thought for me, of putting fur in my mouth, any kind of fur, sets my teeth on edge. For dogs though, being furred creatures themselves you'd think they would find it a breeze; some do, most don't... not initially anyway.

Feathers too can make some dogs gag and not want to have them in their mouths, especially the downy feathers which tend to come out in their mouths and cling to their tongues; got to say it, just writing it is making me wrinkle my face in disgust and making me want to cough and clear my throat.

So let's make it easy for your dog and break him in gently to feather and fur so that holding and retrieving any kind of game is a pleasure for him.

To start your dog on feather you need to get some pheasant wings. If you haven't got access to a couple from a local gamekeeper or the thought of picking up road kill and taking the wings off makes you grimace and go "oh yuck", I'm right there with you. Hi-lost stock pairs of cleaned pheasant wings that you can buy in plastic bags, much easier (see useful contacts), they also do clip on pheasant tails.

Using a half pound softer mouth dummy (remember that by adding complexity in one area you need to reduce it in another) or one of the rugby ball shaped partridge dummies from The Working Dog Company, tie a wing on tightly using some regular string or twine. Keeping it tight to the dummy initially helps to take away the temptation to strip the feathers off it or pick up the dummy and play with it. Once your dog is happily picking this up then add the other wing using strong thread so that when your dog runs with it in his mouth the wing will flap, getting him used to the feel of movement and feathers across his face whilst running.

Ziggy retrieving a half pound dressed dummy

To introduce your dog to fur buy yourself a couple of cured rabbit skins, cut one in half to wrap around a half pound dummy and keep the whole one to attach to a one pound dummy, again using twine. Rabbit skin covered tennis balls are now widely available and are fantastic to use whilst teaching your dog to hunt in short grass.

I tend to use twine initially for dressing dummies as it doesn't affect how a dog picks a dummy up; elastic bands on the other hand may. If I have a dog that is consistently picking a dummy up by an end (not the toggle) then I'll wrap a couple of elastic bands around it so that when the dog picks it up the bands rub across the furry bits of  their lips making them rearrange the dummy so they're holding it in the middle away from the band.

I will also use double sided sticky tape for the same reason, although it's rubbish for attaching feather and fur, it's very good for encouraging a well held dummy with a dog that 'dicks about' with them.

Thinking outside the box

Your retrieve articles shouldn't be restricted to dummies and dressed dummies; gloves, hats, mobile phones and water bottles are all great things to use for retrieving. If your dog doesn't bound as he retrieves, then keys on a large soft key ring are also very good, as if you ever drop your keys you can get your dog to find them. A number of gundog training suppliers are now stocking little canvas dummy shaped key rings – fantastic for training but only if you attach something to them as they're a bit small otherwise.

From phones to remote controls; your dog should retrieve anything you ask him to

Water bottles are especially good and I always train dogs on them as a way of preparing them for going shooting. Why? Well partly because of the size but mainly because you can add water, not only increasing the weight of what they're carrying but also because it moves and sloshes teaching your dog how to carry moving objects; great for preparing them bringing back a live bird that is bobbing its head or moving whilst being carried.

Start with a half litre empty bottle, one that has ridges on it to make it easier for your dog and then build up to a 1.5 litre square shaped one.

When we were doing the photos for this book I couldn't believe that Angus was really struggling to pick up the bottle, it kept sliding out of his mouth and he kept putting it down and rearranging it - he's been retrieving water bottles since he was about eight months!

It was only when I received the photos back from Nick Ridley that I realised I'd used a round, smooth bottle.

Oh Well Done Angus!

Shake...

Water and gundogs go together like... well, water and gundogs. For the most part they love it and some owners find if anything, it's harder to get their dogs out of the water rather than in, however, sometimes it can be too scary a concept for those of a timid disposition. Try to pick a time when the water temperature isn't too cold as if he's chilled afterwards it may put him off.

This is true for experienced dogs as well; earlier this year we were training for the Kennel Club's Working Gundog Certificate and one of the dogs got chilled after a session and refused to go in on the day. He's okay now and loving it again but on the day, which was actually quite warm for the end of February, he went into the lake up to his chest and then refused to budge.

Another dog, following on from a similar experience now wears a neoprene vest for retrieving in water in the winter and she's back to loving the whole thing again, so be warned; if it's too cold, don't train and if you do have to put your dog in, then give him a good towel down as soon as you can and invest in a fleecy coat from somewhere like Equafleece to wick the water away whilst he's in the car on the way home (or between drives if you're on a shoot).

Beanie about to enter the water whilst doing the Kennel Club's Working Gundog Certificate

And bringing back the goods – warm and snug in her neoprene vest

The first thing you need to do is find a good location for your water retrieves as you don't want your dog going out of his depth initially.

Ideally you'll want something that slopes gently into the water with a good bed, not one that moves underneath your dog's paws. You'll want to be able to see the bottom as you need to make sure there's no danger or anything that can put your dog off going in. Oh and make sure you're wearing wellies or waterproofs as the first half a dozen times or so you'll be in the river or the pond with your dog.

'Catch' the dummy if you have to the first couple of times

Stand in the water with your dog to heel and throw the dummy a couple of feet in front of you; an orange puppy dummy is ideal to start with. As soon as it lands send your dog in with a 'get on'. When he picks it up smile and praise him like mad and crouch or bend to take it as he brings it back – all formality is out of the window to start with. Repeat a couple of times and call it a day.

Over the next few retrieves edge yourself closer to the bank for casting off but return to the water for the delivery – the key is to prevent your dog from dropping the dummy; this will start once your dog leaves the water and decides to shake. Dogs rarely shake whilst their paws are in the water but will generally do so once they feel dry land beneath them; their tummies have to be fairly wet to induce a shake but wet ears will produce a shake every time. Whenever your dog shakes, regardless of the circumstances say "shake" so you can turn it into a command; I tend to shake, or rather wiggle, along with my dogs but I know of other trainers that give a hand signal, either moving their hands from side to side or shaking it, as if to shake off water.

Build up your retrieve so that your dog can stand in the shallows with a dummy in his mouth whilst being praised

Keep increasing the distance of either your retrieve into the water or the distance you stand from the water's edge but never do both at the same time.

As you increase the distance that you throw the dummy the more the likelihood is of your dog shaking as he leaves the water so these are the times that you stand with your toes dipped in so that you can take delivery before the shake.

If you mis-time it and your dog drops the dummy just pick it up and put it in his mouth, ask for a nice delivery, praise him and then encourage him to shake.

When your dog is retrieving confidently it's time to try and get the dummy to the other side of the river bank; please check it out first though to make sure it's safe and not scary as you don't want to dent his confidence entering water when you're not around to reassure him.

Just like training steadiness on dry land, now and again you need to go and get the dummy yourself so that your dog doesn't think that every retrieve is for him. If you know or train with friends, then it's a good idea to start some water training as a group; not only does it stretch your dog but if the dummy lands wrong for your dog you can have a more experienced dog bring it back for you. It's also great for teaching steadiness, however, as on dry land, you have to be prepared to get after you dog should the need arise.

I remember one group training session at the water meadows when we sent one dog in for a retrieve and another dog took the opportunity to 'go for it' whilst her handler was distracted chatting to a fellow gundogger. Her owner looked up and started calling for her dog which, as you may have guessed took absolutely no notice - no notice that is until she realised I was running up the river behind her!

As always, never give a command unless you can back it up immediately.

Get over!

It's a good idea to teach your dog to jump whilst holding a dummy. Although jumping comes naturally to dogs, jumping while having something in their mouths doesn't. When a dog jumps his mouth opens or rather, his jaw relaxes and he has to learn to hold on to whatever is in his mouth; hold on to but not damage that is. He also needs to learn how to balance whatever is in his mouth so that it doesn't tip out or catch whatever it is that he's jumping over.

To start off with find a small fallen tree and bounce your dog over it, without a dummy, saying "get over" (or just "over" if you prefer) as he takes off - you've got it, this will associate the action of jumping over something with the command "get over".

Then stand to one side of the log with your dog to heel, making sure you've got a good few feet between you and the log, and throw a dummy to the other side of the log. Send your dog fairly quickly after the dummy lands and as he takes off (both going out and coming back) say "get over". Give him masses of praise.

Once your dog is confident going over the log, heel him out and place the dummy down then return back to your place on the other side of the log and send him so that he's doing a memory retrieve. You can add complexity by building up the distance between you and the log or the log and the dummy; both over time but initially only between one.

Once your dog is happy jumping logs with dummies then it's time to up the ante, and introduce a jumping pen, however, please don't introduce this to Spaniels under ten months and Labradors under twelve as it is quite a strain on their muscles and joints due to the fact that they have to slam their brakes on as soon as they land going in and it's an almost vertical takeoff coming out.

Because, like many other gundog trainers, I rent the ground that I train from, I can't have a permanent jump pen, I really had to think 'outside the box' on how to build one that could go up and down easily and that I could transport; the solution was extendible trellis; you know the stuff that you use in the garden for training climbing plants on. You can fix it into position using plastic stake fencing pins or by making wooden supports; I had the latter made for me but I know some of my handlers use the plastic stakes.

It's great as you can start with it very low and as your dog gets used to jumping in and out you can start to raise the height. Another good feature is that it teaches your dog to jump cleanly rather than try to land on it and then push themselves off, which is what you want in case your dog ever jumps over wire (I know they have to in field trials). Just thinking about what could go wrong with that scenario is making me shiver.

Angus trying to keep the dummy in his mouth on take-off

The down side to the trellis is that it's quite difficult to pin into place and it's rather flimsy which means if your dog catches it whilst jumping over it will make a clatter, however, the flimsiness is one of the things that makes it good as if the dog does clatter into it he won't be overly hurt. Nick Ridley, whilst doing the photos came up with a good idea, and that's to put something like a cane across the top, like a very thin show jumping pole, to make it less scary looking, which is something I'll try out next time I start teaching the jump pen.

As your dog starts to land his bottom jaw automatically opens slightly which is why a lot of dummies are accidently dropped by novice dogs going over obstacles.

It's highly unlikely that you'll retrieve from a jump pen during the natural course of your gundog's working life; it's more likely that you'll do them at scurries or working tests if you decide that's something you'd like to do with your dog. On a shoot however, you may, depending on the terrain that you work your dog on, have to ask your dog to jump out of a tight space with a bird in his mouth; by training for the possibility of it you and your dog will be more confident should the need ever arise.

Bangs and Booms

As a behaviourist I see a lot of dogs that are gun-shy (or in the world away from gundogs 'noise phobic' to gunshot), dogs that haven't been trained as gundogs and never will be; dogs that were, quite simply, in the wrong place at the wrong time with an owner that, reacting out of empathy, gave reassurance thereby praising the fear and escalating it.

As a gundog trainer I see a lot of gun-shy and brain-fried dogs and my heart goes out to the dog and for the most part, but not always, the owner. Why for the most part? Well for the most part it's a case of not knowing - they have a young dog that they've been teaching to retrieve, they're invited out on a local shoot and go for it. If they're lucky the dog doesn't become gun-shy, but if they're unlucky then they can end up with a dog that is a quivering wreck and every time he hears gunfire in the distance ends up shaking, drooling and hiding in his bed; hearing gunfire on walks becomes a disaster as the dog will run in the opposite direction, even if that takes him away from his owner, his home and safety.

Brain-fried dogs are also heart breaking to deal with. The majority of brain-frying occurs the same way that a gun-shy dog is made, out of bad advice and ignorance, but a lot of it happens because owners won't take advice from trainers or experienced 'shooting folk' and introduce their dogs to too much too soon. They may have done a bit of training and have a 'cracking little dog' and go off on their first shoot with the dog not yet a year old. If they're extremely lucky their dog won't be sent into orbit or start barking out of excitement, but listens to his owner and quite often this is true - the first or second time out at least. Once the dog realises just how exciting it all is he won't be able to control his reaction and may end up screaming the place down, spinning round and round on his lead and taking off after everything, not listening to a peep or a scream from his owner; successfully ending his working career.

It really does happen an awful lot, only last month I was teaching basic obedience to a lovely little English Springer Spaniel who was very sweet natured, however as soon as you moved she started pulling and lunging and reacting in a hyperactive manner to any noises she heard. When asking her owner if she was planning on training her as a gundog I was absolutely horrified with her response – she'd already started to clay shoot over her to get her ready for the up and coming season in two and a half months time; the spaniel wasn't even five months old!

Take heed; take your time to introduce the bangs and the booms.

"Hello gun, pleased to meet you"

Introducing a gundog to a gun, or rather a starter pistol, is something that I always plan in advance, although I don't always let the owner know in advance as I don't want to change the training atmosphere. I make sure that as well as having treats and toys available that there's a least one experienced dog around to 'demonstrate' just how much fun it can be. You will need a thrower to help you as you won't be firing the pistol anywhere near your dog.

To start with let your dog sniff the starter pistol, open up the chamber and allow your dog to have a good old sniff. Have your thrower stand about twenty feet away and throw a dummy and fire the empty pistol so that it makes a loud clicking sound, send your dog for the retrieve and give him masses of praise following the delivery. Do this a couple of times and make it fun so that your dog is really keen to go out for the retrieve.

Then have your thrower move back another twenty to thirty feet and throw the dummy a good ten feet towards you and fire a blank at the same time; send your dog once the dummy is down and give loads of praise when your dog brings the dummy back, don't make him sit to deliver the first couple of times and give him a jackpot (three or four treats one after another) once he's at heel.

If you have other dogs around you then keep your dog on lead and let one of the other dogs go first, insist that your dog stays sitting and reward with praise or a sweetie for ignoring the pistol.

End the session without a bang and with a couple of simple retrieves so that your dog ends the training on a high and is really keen for the next one.

If you take it slowly there's no reason for your dog to react negatively to the starter pistol, however, if your dog is timid or worried about noises in general then I would seek expert advice for introducing starter pistols and launchers.

For me taking your time and having fun is what introducing the pistol is all about; can you imagine my horror therefore, when, introducing my youngster to the starter pistol yesterday, he ran over a wasp getting it caught up between his hind legs. He ran towards me proud as punch with a dummy in his mouth and yelped, he then screamed and dropped the dummy and screamed again lifting his right hind off the ground as he flew back to me. Turning him over there was the wasp just to side of his sheath! It was awful and incredibly hard not to make a fuss and baby him. The wasp was killed; Ziggy was rubbed with an antiseptic wipe, sent straight out for simple retrieve, given a jackpot of treats on delivery and then sent out for a dummy with the starter pistol going off. Luckily he's so keen for his retrieves and focussed on the dummy he didn't take any notice of the starter pistol - or his wasp sting for that matter.

"... and you must be the dummy launcher"

There are many types of dummy launchers on the market now, from hand held to remote control and they are all, to my mind, brilliant. If you want to get your dog used to the noise then go for a remote controlled one, similar to those used at scurries, however, if you want to get your dog used to following the line of shot and sitting under a gun then go for a hand held one and attach a stock; whatever you decide to go for though you need to get your dog used to the sound, and it really is a boom rather than a bang.

As always let your dog have a good sniff of the equipment you're going to use; if the equipment is scary to him before it goes boom then you need to forget about using it for a couple of weeks and lay it beside, and then in front of, his food bowl so that he realises there's nothing to worry about – remember to move it around every couple of days so that he gets used to seeing it in different places.

To start off with you'll only use starter pistol blanks in the launcher so that it makes more of a 'pop' on launching, that way you can get your dog used to the extra equipment and, if you have a launcher with a stock, used to seeing your thrower raise it up to their shoulder.

When your dog is happy with the popping sound then it's time to use the launcher blanks. They come in three strengths; green is the shortest distance, then yellow followed by red - and they really do go a fair distance, especially if you use a solid dummy rather than a canvas one.

Regardless of whether you're using a hand-held or a remote launcher, the first time you use the launcher blanks you need to be at distance. If you think of the clock (and it should be a huge one), position yourself and your dog at 6 o'clock with the launcher at 4 o'clock, that way you're between the dog and the launcher and will protect him slightly from the sound, also your launcher is slightly ahead of you so the sound won't be so deafening for your dog - remember whoever uses the launcher needs ear protectors (defenders).

Angus at 6, the launcher at 4;
I would be standing with Angus
for the retrieve

For the first retrieve, as soon as the dummy lands send your dog so he associates the boom with the retrieve and therefore fun. As your dog becomes confident then make him wait for the retrieve, or heel him away and back again.

When he is confident with the sound you can then put him to heel as you use the launcher, however as with extending any training exercise, increase one element at a time only so, for example the first time you use the launcher with him to heel, you would only launch one dummy rather than doing a couple in a row.

When you first start to use the launcher blanks, pick your training ground carefully; when I introduced Angus to the launcher I didn't; to be perfectly honest it didn't even enter my head. We used to live round the corner from a fantastic field which was separated from Marlborough Football Club with a wire fence and well spaced trees. It was a Sunday afternoon, a reasonably nice day and neither myself nor my hubby had any plans "fancy helping me introduce Angus to the launcher?", "yeah, okay".

So off we went, dummy bag, hand held launcher, launcher blanks, launcher dummies and treats. Kenny stood parallel to the fence and I moved off to put a bit of distance between us. BANG! Sent Angus, off he went and did a nice retrieve, delivered to hand, put him to heel, gave him a couple of treats and turned to Kenny with a beaming smile on my face and my jaw dropped. Everyone, the supporters, the referee and the players, had stopped what they were doing and were looking at us! Yes, it really does make that much noise.

And finally, the only other thing you need to remember about training with your launcher, and it is a drag, is to occasionally go and collect the dummy yourself otherwise your dog will think that every dummy that you launch is for him - and, just in case you missed it the first time round; the green launcher blanks don't go as far as the red or the yellow ones...

Smile for the Birdie!

You've already started to introduce feather using dressed dummies, now it's time to introduce your dog to a dead bird. Until you go on a shoot you'll only be able to use cold birds that are slightly stiff - unfortunately this means that there will be another learning process when you go on a shoot. However, it's worth doing so that your dog gets used to the weight, the feathers and the smell.

If you're never going to take your dog shooting then you can skip this bit as it really is all about introducing birds and I totally understand if this isn't something that you want to do.

Before moving to New Zealand I hadn't really done much work with birds, preferring to train for working tests that, in the UK, are run on dummies (and occasionally cold game in preparation for the trialling season). In New Zealand however, the puppy tests end when the dog is a year old and thereafter all tests are on dead pigeons. I really didn't enjoy having pigeons wrapped in newspaper in my freezer and stopped being involved with gundogs for a while; however, I missed it terribly and ended up going back and competing. It's changed a lot since I lived there and they have since had their first pheasant shoots and field trials on live birds.

A pigeon is a good sized bird for your dog to hold first, however, the feathers on their breast are very fine and downy and can put a lot of dogs off as the feathers stick to their tongues. The way around this is to put the bird into a stocking. I prefer to start with two layers of regular tights (15 or 20 denier); put the first leg over the bird and make a cut in the stocking so that you can pull a wing out; when you put the second leg on leave the wing inside.

Let your dog have a good sniff. When he's finished sniffing he'll either try to put it in his mouth or walk away; at that point tell him to hold the bird in the same way that you would get him to hold a dummy. Praise him like mad and throw the bird for him and as it lands send him for it. When he gets there he might give it a good sniff again and try to figure out what it is and how to hold it. It's really important at this point you allow him time to process things and not call him off the bird; once he picks it up praise him all the way back, allow a stand delivery and praise him again.

Initially allow your dog some mental space to figure out what he has to do with the bird ...

If he heads back without the bird, then make a game of it as you would have done when he was a youngster and was unsure of how to pick up a big dummy, throw it and send him at the same time, keeping your tone of voice light and easy.

... with patience and a bit of luck, you'll be rewarded with a retrieve.

After a couple of retrieves you can remove the outer stocking so that there is a wing free and then, when your dog is used to retrieving with a flapping wing, rather than remove the stocking completely I'd just free up the other wing.

If you have access to pheasants then a small hen bird dressed in a single stocking with one or both wings free is an excellent place to start and wherever possible this is where I begin. After you've used the bird for the day, wrap it in newspaper then in a carrier bag and freeze it. Defrost it overnight for further use; if you do this you may get two or three really good training sessions per bird. When you've finished with it put it out of the way in the forest or off the beaten track so that another animal may eat and the bird hasn't been wasted.

Recent additions to the equipment you can buy (from Hi-Lost) are pheasant dummies; they are quite literally skinned pheasants sewn onto a canvas dummy. They make a good introduction to birds if you don't have any birds available, however, they are quite expensive as far as dummies go and I wouldn't want them to get wet as I expect the feathers wouldn't last too long. When I introduced them at training, the 'old hands' that had been shooting had a sniff and their faces looked as if they were thinking "you want me to put that in my mouth – it's neither one thing nor the other", the younger, inexperienced dogs couldn't believe their luck and got very excited, however, once they were thrown, the older dogs 'came alive' and had a great time hunting them out in the forest.

I believe that these dummies could have some benefit for rehabbing wayward gundogs, of which I've seen a number, but none since the dummies came out so I haven't had the chance to try it out yet. These are the dogs that want to eat the bird that they retrieve and will slink off under a bush with their prize, or dogs that clamp down on a bird and refuse to hand it over without a fight or mouthing (munch) it.

As always with your training, once your dog his happy going out then insist on a tidy delivery and remember to collect the bird yourself occasionally.

Training two

I found writing this section really difficult to start; I had it in my head that I would be using photos of Bart and Angus to demonstrate putting two dogs together during training but sadly Bart died in the August following publication of The Pet Gundog. I was devastated, he taught me so much both how to do it and how not to do it and, almost a year to the day later, I still miss him terribly. I see glimpses of him in his nephew, the young black lab lying at my feet, but thankfully Ziggy is very much his own dog and so the memories of Bart stay intact and don't get blurred or overly confused.

For the photo shoot Darren, one of my handlers, very kindly allowed me to use Moss, his wonderful yellow Labrador alongside Angus; although we did the photos, I have to say it was with a very heavy heart.

If you find yourself in the lucky position of living with two gundogs then you also find yourself in the unlucky position of having to train two gundogs. Why unlucky? Well, when you bring in the youngster you have to do two lots of everything; two lots of walking, two lots of training and two lots of one to one time. You then, at some point, have to take a deep breath and put the dogs together to walk, train and hopefully work.

Forget about doing any kind of gundog training when you first put your dogs together and concentrate on all the basic obedience exercises that I ran through in gundogs 101 at the beginning of the book. To start off with it's easier to put your older dog on one side and your youngster on the other; 'side' is the command that I use when I want my dogs to walk on my right, 'heel' is on my left. To start with all you do is put your dog on your right and say "side, good boy" and talk to him when you're walking; every now and again give him a treat when he's in the correct position. Don't get growly or angry with him, just calmly put him back using your lead to guide him. This command is also great if you're walking into traffic on country lanes as you can tuck your dogs on to the verge.

So walk with your dogs for a couple of weeks with one on either side; it will help to eliminate the competition of one dog trying to get in front of the other, which will happen when they're on the same side. When they're walking nicely like this, put them both on the same side for heel walking. Although in the pack the most senior rank walks closest to the leader, I tend to put the

Start off by having both of your dogs sitting facing you, then call one dog.

So...
Moss, sit; Angus come

Quietly praise and then reverse the commands.

So... Angus, sit; Moss come

youngster closer to me as being the closest makes it easier to keep him in the heel position; once they can walk nicely together then I just say "heel" and let them sort out the position themselves, which is very interesting and very telling about your pack.

Bart always used to walk closest with Angus on the outside (once I let them choose their own position); I've been letting Angus and Ziggy choose their positions the last month or so and Angus is staying on the outside which is really interesting, especially as we've had a couple of Mexican standoffs in doorways recently.

Early on I establish command on name, so for example when I let them out of the back door, I'll open the door and say the dog's name that I wish to go out; I'll sometimes prefix it with "not you", especially in the early days of training it, so it would be "not you Ziggy, Angus out" and so on - you get the picture don't you.

I spend a lot of time with the dogs sitting in front a couple of feet away and calling one by name, having them sit in front of me and then calling the other.

I progress this to doing it on the move; I'll heel the dogs and tell one to sit and continue walking with the other. Initially I'll call the sitting dog to heel, walk for a few strides and then tell the other dog to sit and repeat the exercise, however, once they become proficient I'll sit one dog, then sit the other and then call the first dog past the sitting dog and into the heel position. So it goes like this.

"Dogs, heel" ('dogs' is a term I use when I'm addressing both dogs, saves me shouting both of their names), and walk for a little way.
"Ziggy, sit" and continue on heeling Angus.
"Angus, sit" and continue on a few strides without a dog.
"Ziggy, heel" keep walking for a few strides after Ziggy has caught up.
"Ziggy, sit" and continue on a few strides without a dog.
"Angus, heel" keep walking for a few strides after Angus has caught up.
"Ziggy, heel".

It looks so impressive and I used to do it at demonstrations with Bart and Angus to show how you can train your dog regardless of what's happening around him.

When you can call your dogs past each other they're ready and steady enough to retrieve side by side. Sit your dogs to heel, tell them to wait and walk out with a dummy, placing it about ten feet or so in front of your dog. Return to their side and say "not you" to the dog that is staying put and then send the other. So in this situation I said "not you Moss, Angus get on".

As your dog returns with the dummy tell the dog at heel to stay to prevent any moving or mobbing of the dog coming in with the dummy and encourage a nice delivery by stepping back and inviting your dog into your space. Finish by putting your dog to heel and repeat the exercise for the other dog by leaving the first one where he is and bringing your second dog into the heel position; basically the dog closest to your leg gets the retrieve.

"not you Moss; Angus get on"

As your dogs become more proficient and you become more confident with your handling of two dogs (a brace), you can send either dog for the retrieve and start to be inventive with it.

One of the things I train my advanced handlers (as well as doing it with my own dogs) is to send their dog for a dummy and stop him half way, we then send another dog past the sitting dog for the retrieve; once the dog has delivered and is sitting nicely to heel we throw a dummy behind us and send the sitting dog past us with a 'get on' - all great stuff and takes your dog's steadiness to another level!

Where do we go from here?

You now have all the training techniques you need to branch out in to the big wide world of some serious 'gundogging', the choice of which path, or paths, that you go down is up to you.

I outlined the various things that you can do with your dog in The Pet Gundog and so rather than go over the technicalities again I thought I'd take a different approach and give you the 'how to train for' or at least nudge you in the right direction instead.

Training days and workshops

These can be fantastic and very beneficial as you get to learn about different approaches to the same exercise and draw on other trainers' experiences and training techniques. A lot of gundog trainers that I know, myself included, run training days covering everything from an introduction to gundog training and a return to the basics (something we all need to do on a regular basis), to advanced techniques and water training, to introducing shot and preparing for the shooting season.

Whenever I run a training day I try to make it clear that if there is an exercise that I teach and you don't want to do it then you don't have to, for example playing pull with your dog and using toys in training. If I try to improve a technique and all I meet is constant resistance however, then I must admit, I start to wonder why the person is there at all. If you attend training days, be open-minded, be prepared to learn and be inspired and, if you don't want to do a technique, speak up, however if you totally disagree with everything the trainer is saying and doing then I would make an excuse and exit at the next break.

I quite often encourage handlers to go to training days as a spectator, especially if they want to broaden their knowledge without necessarily changing their techniques or if they don't feel confident about going with their dog; the majority of trainers will allow a certain number of spectators at a reduced rate.

Remember a good trainer should be able to tell you not only how to do something but why they want you do it and more importantly why it works.

Trainer hopping

If you're not happy with your trainer you need to do something about it, but before you take the plunge and leave you should be asking yourself some questions; the most obvious one being "why not?"

Is it because the group isn't going fast enough (in which case look at doing one to one training), you don't enjoy the group or the timing is wrong (in which case try to change groups), or you're not happy with the training techniques being used. For any of these I would recommend that you talk to your trainer about it first and see if you can come up with a solution.

I only train during the day mid-week, so I'm always more than happy to recommend other trainers if my training timetable doesn't suit people who ask to train with me. I'm also happy to recommend other trainers for things like specialised HPR or field trial training.

If you're thinking of changing trainer because you clash or because your trainer is too hard on your dog, or you, then bite the bullet and find someone else.

Generally though, going from one trainer to another is a bad idea. You'll be given lots of different training techniques, quite often contradicting each other and not only will you get confused but so will your dog, you'll also miss out on continuity and consistency and end up with gaps in yours and your dog's education.

This is where training days and workshops come into their own as they give you a chance to 'taste and try before you buy' or at least commit to changing trainers; you also get to hear the same thing in a different way which can make a difference to how you perceive something allowing the 'niggle' to be resolved.

(I was really hoping that the resolution of a niggle was noggled, but it isn't (although it should be) and so we'll have to make do with 'resolved', or until such times, of course, as the Oxford English Dictionary accepts 'noggled'.)

Scurries

Scurries are great fun and a lot of my handlers do one or two over the summer as a way of getting out and about with their dogs and their families. They're all well aware that they need to still insist on good delivery to hand and if it goes pear shaped on the day to turn it into a training exercise. They've all put so much effort into training their dogs they don't want to undo all that hard work.

And scurries can; they're exciting, it's against the clock and you get caught up in the moment (especially if you have a fast dog). I'm all in favour of them and have had many weekend phone calls from handlers over the last few years giving me updates on how they're doing.

If you're serious about scurrying then you need to get your dog really fit and do lots of sporadic retrieving on your walks. This is where you need to concentrate your efforts; fitness and speed, not just on retrieving the dummy but on bringing it back as well. An accurate delivery is a must but don't make the mistake of snatching the dummy from your dog's mouth as not only is it uncomfortable for your dog, but it will put him off giving it up and he may start turning his head away from you; the exact opposite of what you want!

Get used to working your dog from a box, either imaginary or by making one with four leads placed down; send your dog from the front of the box and as he starts coming back scoot to the back so that he's still running flat out as he crosses the line, and hopefully stops the clock. It will also help you to realise where you are in relation to your dog as if you step outside of the box in a competition you will be eliminated.

Remember to keep upping the ante on your training with your dog, especially if you're aiming for the high stake scurries.

The Kennel Club's Working Gundog Certificate

The Kennel Club tried to come up with an assessment for registered pedigree gundogs that says they're ready for the shoot but without it being a competition. I think it's a great idea and anything that gets you training your dog works for me.

Another really cool thing about it is that when you pass you are presented with your certificate at Crufts. Because you can get your working gundog certificate for working on dummies I think it's perfect for people who want to train their dog to a high standard but aren't into competing or want to go shooting.

If you've worked your way through this book, taken your time and trained in a group for steadiness on retrieving, then you'll be ready to do your Working

Gundog Certificate which consists of a simulated drive, a water retrieve, retrieving over a small jump and a steadiness test; all you need to do is to find one that is being run in your area, or close to and on the retrieve items you're interested in, either dummies or game. If you have a dog that points then there are specialised certificate days for you too.

Then log on to Google Earth or Google Maps, or use ordinance survey maps, and try to figure out the lay of the land and train accordingly; if the area is surrounded by trees then do some training in the forest, doing both marked and blind retrieves and hunt your dog amongst the ferns; if the area is open then concentrate working in the open, doing long retrieves and hunting along hedges and fence lines.

The key though will be training in as many different places as possible to raise your confidence in your dog's ability to be able to work when you arrive at the venue.

Tests and Trials

If you want to do working tests or field trials then I can't recommend highly enough that you join a club so that you're interacting with people who are hopefully, competing with their dogs. If you want to do the competition circuit then you have to see and be seen. There are many around, some that are specific to an area and some that have branches all around the country. The best way to find your local gundog club is through the Kennel Club's website which lists all affiliated clubs.

Check out the club over the phone, have a chat with the secretary and preferably a couple of the trainers and ask if you can go along to watch without your dog, or take your dog and join in half way through. Most club training isn't run at the same level, pace or depth as going to professional gundog trainer's classes, however the trainers should still be able to tell you why they want you to do something and not just 'because this is how the trialers do it'.

If you can't find a club in your area then think about setting up a training group/practice sessions with friends or maybe with people you meet at working tests and start training towards them; you have the 'how to' as well as the 'why' in this book, now it's a case of thinking outside the box and practicing in lots of different locations and having other people to throw dummies for you.

Once my handlers are at a certain level, I encourage them to join various clubs so that they can see what else is happening in the gundog world; it also means that they get to bring back different techniques to class that we can then discuss the merits of (or not as the case may be) as well as the different handling skills.

When you join a club training group you're looking for the same qualities in the club trainer as you are in a professional gundog trainer; knowledge, patience, humour, common sense and no harsh handling or demeaning the handlers. Years ago I can remember the stinging remark of "just 'cos you've got the wellies and the hat doesn't mean you're a gundog trainer"; good natured bantering and mickey taking is great as it leads to group bonding... ridicule isn't.

I covered harsh handling in The Pet Gundog so won't revisit that ground again, but there is a difference between applying discipline appropriately in an appropriate and timely manner and harsh handling; the former is necessary the latter should be frowned upon whether that is a gundog trainer, a field trialist or a handler at class doing it.

Competing

No-one can really prepare you for your first working test or field trial as the adrenaline will be pumping on the day and you'll feel totally overwhelmed to start off with; hopefully after the second exercise you'll be able to start relaxing and enjoying it. If you get put out of your first field trial or have a zero mark on one of your working test exercises, look on the positive side, you now have something to concentrate on at training.

The first time you are placed you won't be able to stop smiling and will end up with seriously sore 'smug' muscles; you'll spend your evening searching for more clubs to join and more competitions to enter. Unfortunately dogs are such great levellers, it won't be long before you find fault with your training again.

For a seriously competitive person, tests and trials funnily enough, just don't seem to do it for me. I've tried a number of times competing my dogs, both here in the UK and in NZ but something just didn't click for me; I prefer getting inside my dog's head, figuring out what makes him tick and training him accordingly. I would much rather go out with my advanced handlers and have fun pushing the dogs that little bit further, than to have someone judge my dog over a couple of retrieves and give me some well meaning advice. That's not to say I don't encourage others from competing, as I do, and we tailor the training in class to cater for the working test and scurry season.

The people I've met here and abroad whilst out on the circuit have been really friendly; they all know what it's like to train in torrential rain on a cold winters morning and so there tends to be a lot of camaraderie while waiting for your turn. Ziggy, my youngster, is a seriously good dog and so who knows, when I do a working test with him next year I may well change my mind and think I'll take him trialling after a season or two picking up, however, for now, I think I'll stick with shooting.

Going Shooting

Talking about changing your mind... one of my handlers has been training with me for a couple of years, first of all for her Kennel Club Good Citizen Awards and then for gundog training. Right from the off it was a case of she would never take her dog on a shoot, she just wanted a well trained dog that she could have some fun with and keep occupied and so she wasn't always quite so hot on making her dog do what she wanted and her commands and hand signals weren't quite as crisp as they could have been.

Then, last season, she went shooting and absolutely loved it. Within a week she decided she wanted to take her dog out picking up, then, by the end of the season she decided she wanted a peg dog - oh boy! It was a case of back to basics and tightening everything up for a good picking up dog this season, peg dog next.

I thought it was fantastic that my handler changed her mind and wanted to take her dog shooting, her dog is awesome, so enthusiastic and biddable; I just wish she'd decided before she started letting the serious stuff get a bit sloppy. So, be warned! Whether you think you'll take your dog shooting or not, train him to the best of your ability and train as if you're going to be going on the best shoot there is. When I teach people to train their dogs as gundogs I always have in my mind the shoot that I pick up at in the New Forest and try to get them to a level that if they did ever get to go out on it they would always be invited back.

Half the battle for you as a new 'gundogger' is finding a shoot that you can go on; asking your trainer if they'll take you out is a great idea (I use a small local syndicate shoot as a training shoot which is fantastic), failing that you could contact The British Association for Shooting and Conservation (BASC) or the National Organisation of Beaters and Pickers Up (NOBs) for information on shoots in your area (see useful contacts at the back of this book). You should also be looking to join one of these organisations (or both) to make sure you're sufficiently insured before you take part.

Once you've found yourself a shoot you need to tailor your dog's training to suit it; this is true whether you beat or pick-up. I go picking up mainly in the New Forest and so concentrate throughout September in brushing up Angus' forest skill; we also do mock drives in training using starter pistols and have the dogs working together as we would on a shoot as it's very different to standing in line taking turns on your retrieve. One of the many reasons why some of the earlier techniques have recommended training with friends and other dogs is that a shoot can be a very busy place.

Darren & Moss work as a picking up team

As a picker-up I stand at the back out of the way with my dog to heel (and on lead for the most part).

When the 'end of shooting' whistle goes then it's a case of releasing Angus (who will insist on giving one loud woof the first time he's released on the first drive of the day), pointing him in the right direction and sending him on – his nose will pick up the scent and bring home a bird.

Angus is also experienced enough now to be sent for a runner (a bird that is shot but not killed outright and is on the move) and so may be sent before the shoot captain gives the all clear to release the picking up dogs.

As a Beater you need to find out from the shoot captain or gamekeeper what is expected of you as well as the terrain that you're going to be working in. Some shoots allow beaters to take their dogs with them, others don't; some allow the beaters dogs to be off lead, others don't; some of the smaller shoots don't have pickers-up but rely on the beaters dogs to pick up any shot birds.

It really is a case of training your dog as an all round gundog and then when he's trained, adapting your training and your dog's skills for the terrain and conditions that you're going to be working him in.

If, after a season of picking-up, you've decided that as you shoot, you would like your dog on the peg with you, then over the spring and summer months take some time out to change your dogs working position from sitting at your left leg to sitting a couple of paces in front of you; this is where the steadiness of sitting in front following a delivery is going to pay dividends.

Going back to the starter pistol blanks in a launcher on a stock, pop your dog a couple of paces in front of you so that you're facing each other. Raise your stock as if you're aiming for a bird and swing around so you turn away from your dog and fire the launcher at the same time as saying "mark". Lower your launcher and send your dog past you for the retrieve; build up to doing two or three launches before sending your dog to pick up for you.

When your dog is steady to the 'pop' of the launcher, you need to start using the launcher blanks, building up the complexity in exactly the same way; but be aware that shooting over the top of your dog a lot will cause deafness over time so be considerate with your training.

Your first shoot will be nerve-racking, but everyone remembers theirs and how out of their depth they felt and will take you under their wing; the beaters will keep you amused with their own particular sense of humour (I dread to think what my 14 year old son learned when he came out with us on his first beat a couple of years ago; I still haven't asked) and if you're picking up you'll be paired up with someone experienced who can talk you through the proceedings and any quirks of that particular drive.

Just take your time, don't over face your dog. For the first couple of drives keep him on lead and let him soak up the atmosphere, keeping him calm and quiet and allowing him a sniff of the birds before they go in the game cart. If you're picking up, then at the end of the second or third drive introduce him to a warm bird in the same way you did with cold game; a sniff, a hold and short retrieve with

masses of praise - keep it calm, keep it quiet, keep it relaxed and keep it easy and it won't take your dog long to understand what is expected of him.

I remember my first shoot after coming home from New Zealand; and I still cringe! Bart and Angus went to stay with my friend Jill, who runs the picking up team at the New Forest shoot that I pick up at and who also bred Bart and Ziggy. The dogs had been there for two weeks before we arrived at around seven o'clock at night. Following on from a quick hello and a big cuddle the dogs were settled for the night. The next morning it was up and ready for the shoot; Bart was totally wired as he hadn't seen me forever and he was going shooting! The alarm bells should have rang but they didn't. Anyway, we were standing under the trees when we spotted a runner.

Jill asked if Bart had marked it; he had so she said I could send him. Now Bart was good – this is a dog that was placed first time out in a field trial, however, at that moment in time he wasn't my dog; I hadn't seen him for two weeks and I hadn't made him my own again through training prior to going on the shoot - well he was off, straight past the runner, straight past the guns heading towards the beating line; I can still hear, quite clearly the Shoot Captain telling me to get my dog under control. Even writing this now, years later, I get a sinking feeling in the bottom of my stomach.

Take heed, it doesn't matter how good your dog is, if you've been separated from him before a shoot don't send him for a runner; if you don't think you have a dog working on the whistle, don't send him for a runner; if you are at all unsure, *don't send him for a runner* – it could not only wreak havoc on the current drive for everyone but if your dog crosses a hedge line it could wreck the next one as well.

The Pheasant Shoot

Preparing for the season

Whilst all pheasant shoots are different, or rather run in different ways, the cycle of the shoot and the shooting year is more or less the same. All that really changes is the timing of it, which is dependent upon the age of the birds that are being reared (or bought in) and when it is intended for them to be released, which can be any time from June until approximately early August.

More and more shoots are now buying in seven week old Pheasant Poults from game farms which are delivered straight into their release pens. Buying in poults is not so labour intensive and so frees up the keepers, over about a three month period, to carry out other Estate work, for example fencing and forestry, which reduces the shoot running costs.

This is the alternative to running a laying flock, where the Head gamekeeper and his team are responsible for catching sufficient Hens and Cocks at the end of the shooting season and holding them in net covered pens so as they can gather the eggs for incubation. The resulting chicks, when hatched, are then transferred to the rearing field where they are raised to seven weeks old before being transferred to the release pens. A release pen, which is a secure fenced area within the Estate/Farm woodlands and resembles an over grown chicken run, is used to acclimatise young birds to a woodland environment, protect them from predators and to get them used to the drinking and feeding system that will be used across the shoot after their release.

Regardless of whether the birds are bought in or hand reared, at around twelve weeks of age the young pheasants are gradually released into the surrounding woodland and game covers, which is an area of farm land that is planted with maize or other crops to create an area (often covering several acres) from which the birds are driven over the guns from in the shooting season.

Once the birds are released the Keepers main purpose in life is to ensure that they remain on the ground and in the areas that are used to hold them in for shoot days; this being achieved by ensuring that there is sufficient food and water available to them at all times, gently pushing them back into the area from the boundaries with their dogs on a daily basis (referred to as dogging in) and controlling predators.

All pheasants need to be fully grown, which is around the age of 21 weeks, prior to be included in any shooting programme; the Pheasant shooting season runs from October 1st until February 1st inclusive and the Partridge season from September 1st until January 31st.

Shoot days are planned far in advance as, on the bigger commercial shoots, more than one days shooting could be taking place in the same week! This means ensuring that all of the gun pegs are in place, picking up spent cartridges from previous days, ensuring that sufficient Beaters, Pickers up, Game cart operator and Loaders (if required) are able to attend and that the shoot transport has sufficient fuel and is road worthy. And yes, all of the shoot health and safety policies, backed by the various risk assessments have to be available and up-to-date.

As you might guess, the shoot day is the end product of many months of hard work on the part of the keeper and his unsung support team.

The shooting day

The shoot day generally consists of five or six drives where, under the direction of the Head keeper, the beating team would drive the birds to a flushing point from where they would be lifted to fly over the guns that are standing on strategically positioned gun stands within the woodland or in front of a game cover.

As the drive progresses the pickers up come into their own, working their dogs mainly on runners (wounded birds) whilst the drive is going on so that they can be humanely dispatched once retrieved.

At the end of the drive they can then sweep the area behind and in front of the guns for dead birds, while at the same time ensuring that any gun which has brought his own dog along is left sufficient birds behind his peg to pick up himself. Not only is this a common courtesy but, it must be remembered, that this person, The Gun, has paid a substantial sum of money for the day and has brought his own dog to enjoy working him.

Once all of the birds are collected they are braced (paired up) and hung on the game cart to cool prior to being transported to the game larder/chillier for either collection by a registered game dealer or for processing in house. All dead birds need to be handled and treated with respect as they are not only an end product of the shoot, but also destined for the human food chain.

This process continues until the end of the season on February 1st when the keepering team hopefully get to take a well deserved holiday; the beaters, pickers up and other support staff should all have been properly thanked and provided with, hopefully, an end of season party and one or two days shooting to reduce the amount of Cock pheasants left on the ground, and, if everything has gone according to plan, the Head keeper/Shoot manager should already have repeat bookings for the next season so that it can start all over again!

The Shoot and its importance to the rural community

I remember years ago standing in my friend's office looking at this picture thinking it was just fantastic. I probably knew on some level just how many people were involved in the shoot one way or another, but to see it drawn in this simplistic yet detailed way was just magic.

It's now out of print and no longer available, however, The Countryside Alliance very kindly allowed me to take an electronic version of my friend's poster; I hope you enjoy poring over it as much as I have over the years.

Out and About

I was out training the other week with a couple of friends in the fields around where I live; it's a great area for training as not only are there mown walkways but there are also strips of long grass, dirt tracks across fields and through bushes, perfect for all levels of gundog training.

I was standing at the bottom of the hill in the short grass and my friends were at the top of the hill; when it was my turn to go they threw the dummy around the other side of the strip of long grass but still on the mown bit. I sent Angus and he ran so far along the strip, then jumped in and started hunting in the long grass, about thirty feet short of the mark; I pushed him back a couple of times but he didn't want to leave the long grass. He was having such a good time as this is normally where he frolics around on our walks, however, he was meant to be working! "Get out of there Angus" I hollered, sure enough out he came. I was then able send him back alongside the strip rather than though it.

Both my friends just looked at me; "how did you do that, how do you train it?" I looked at them just as incredulously and replied "when I tell him to get out of a room", "oh yeah...." was the response.

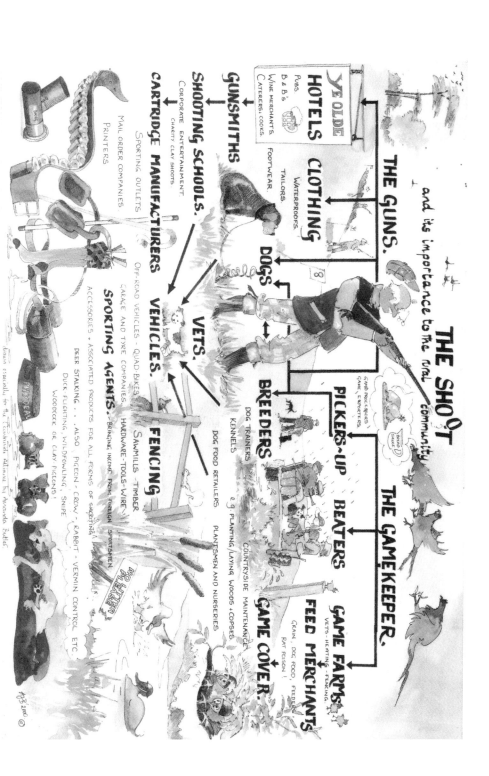

and its importance to the rural community

THE SHOOT

THE GUNS.

HOTELS
Pubs
B & B's
Wine merchants.
Caterers, cooks.

CLOTHING
Waterproofs.
Tailors.
Footwear.

GUNSMITHS

SHOOTING SCHOOLS.
Corporate entertainment.
Charity clay shoots.

CARTRIDGE MANUFACTURERS
Mail order companies.
Printers
Sporting outlets

DOGS

VETS.

VEHICLES.
Off-road vehicles - quad bikes.
Garage and tyre companies.

SPORTING AGENTS.
Hardware - tools - wire.
Bringing income from foreign sportsmen.

Accessories • associated products for all forms of shooting.
Deer stalking . . . also pigeon - crow - rabbit - vermin control etc.
Duck-flighting, wildfowling, snipe
Woodcock or clay pigeons!

FENCING
Sawmills - timber

THE GAMEKEEPER.

PICKERS-UP

BEATERS

BREEDERS
Dog trainers
Kennels
Dog food retailers

e.g. Planting/laying woods + copses.
Countryside maintenance.
Plantsmen and nurseries.

Game processors,
Game experts.

GAME FARMS

FEED MERCHANTS
Grain, dog food, feeders.
Rat poison!
Vets - heating - fencing.

GAME COVER.

Drawn especially for the Countryside Alliance by Amanda Rahtz

We are constantly training our dogs, whether we realise it or not, especially when they live indoors with us. Just think of all the things you say that your dog responds to; "get in" or "in" or "in you go" are all things that I say to my dogs if I want them to go into a room ahead of me (yes I know, very consistent with my commands huh? At least 'in' is used each time); "out", "come out", "get out of there" are all things that I say if I want my dogs to leave the room or go out of a room ahead of me.

Another command that I use is "get up" (and the variants, "up", "up you get") which is for putting my dogs in the back of my car, however, I have used it to send a dog to a higher position on a retrieve – so up a step or to jump up onto a ledge or bank.

When you're working your dog at distance and you're not quite sure how to get him to do something, put him in a sit using your whistle, take a breath and a moment or two to think about similar situations you found yourself in and how you dealt with it, like Angus not leaving the strip of long grass for example.

When you're out and about with your dogs, walking them or driving with your dogs in the car, keep an eye out for retrieving and hunting opportunities; a nice dirt track alongside the edge of a field, a strip of long grass, a fallen tree and so on, anything to stretch your dog and your handling skills a little bit further. And remember, it doesn't have to be a difficult exercise; an exercise that you've done a hundred times at home, when done in a new place is, in effect, a new exercise.

However, it's not all about going for the next retrieve and constantly pushing yourself; it's about leadership. It's about building a relationship with your dog based on trust and respect; it's about having a well-mannered, well-behaved dog that you can take to the local pub or to the shooting field; it's about having a companion at your side that you can be proud of; it's about enjoying your dog and having fun.

And so, as I say to my handlers when I'm not going to see them for a wee while... take it easy, stay safe, have fun and happy gundogging!

A Rose by any other name...

I was going to add a formal glossary of terms to the end of this book, however, the terms that I use like "go BACK" for example, may mean something else to other trainers as we all tend to use the terms that suit us, or rather that suited the trainers that we originally trained with.

Other words we use fit into the circumstances of our lives at the time; many gundog folk will use the word 'dead', which is a command you give your dog to hand over the bird, or the dummy, that is in his mouth; I use 'give' because when I was training Bart initially as a gundog my son was still very young and I didn't like the thought of him running around saying 'dead' all of the time.

Again, I use 'find it' rather than 'hi-lost' to mean 'get your head down and use your nose' because I wanted my son to play hide and seek with toys around the house with Bart and it was a good command for a seven year old to use. We also used to let my son hide behind trees in the forest and get Bart to 'find' him, by tracking his scent; not quite a blind retrieve but great training for a gundog.

I thought about adding shooting terms that you may come across but then thought that a lot of the terms that I've used I've explained at the time of using them. Also, if I added them for you, you would miss out on interacting with people on the shoot, or the working test or the field trial, as hopefully they'll not only explain what the thing is but will share their own stories with you. An example of this is when I asked what the cosh was called that they use on a shoot to dispatch the birds. I was told "a Priest" - shortly followed by a growly voice that said "it's 'cos we use it to administer the last rites Lez"

My advice then, in relation to the various terminologies you're going to hear bandied about, is to ask what it means. By all means look it up in books or on the internet if you don't want to appear ignorant but then use the information you've found as verification with the old hands out there; you'll no doubt get a greater understanding by asking and, hopefully, you'll get a story or three thrown in.

About the Author

Lez Graham works full-time as a canine behaviour practitioner and gundog trainer, is the Education & Development Officer for the Guild of Dog Trainers and is a tutor with the Cambridge Institute of Dog Behaviour & Training.

A dog behaviour specialist with a penchant for gundogs, Lez runs weekly gundog training classes and specialised gundog training days. As a gundog trainer, Lez focuses on steadiness and obedience and, by bringing the behaviour element into her gundog training, her handlers get a deeper understanding of why we train the gundog the way we do. Moving away from the 'old-style/traditional' gundog training and yet keeping the discipline of the well trained field dog; she encourages play and touch to facilitate a strong bond between dog and handler.

Lez has competed in Working Tests in the United Kingdom, Gundog Field Tests in New Zealand, competition obedience and 'works' her gundogs during the shooting season.

Lez is one of only three people in the UK to achieve an MA Professional Practice (Canine Behaviour & Psychology), she is a full member of the Canine and Feline Behaviour Association (CFBA) and is a Master Trainer with the Guild of Dog Trainers (GoDT).

Lez lives in Wiltshire with her husband, her son and her two gundogs.

My Masters degree

MA Professional Practice (Canine Behaviour & Psychology)

Right from tagging along with Bart's breeder to my first shoot, when Bart was about six months old (and left at home I hasten to add), I've been hooked. I remember so clearly standing under a tree with my friend watching Bart's mum go after a runner. It really made me appreciate the need for having picking up dogs on a shoot. Watching Willow run after a bird with her mouth wide open and then gently scooping it up before slamming on the brakes and returning to Jill was just pure magic and made me go 'wow'. It was then that I decided I was going to train Bart as a gundog.

My fascination hasn't dimmed, if anything over time it's burned brighter and I still get those heart stopping moments of pride and pure joy at training; whether it's watching and waiting for my youngster to come round a bend with a retrieve that I sent him back for a few minutes ago, or watching a new handler's face as they get delivery to hand for the first time.

The behaviour element of gundog training is the bit that I love the most; getting inside another species head and figuring out what makes it tick is just awesome.

To be able to train a predator to ignore its instinct and not chase the bird on the ground until permission is given, to not slink off under the tree with a warm and tasty snack in the shape of a freshly shot bird, to not mouth and chew 'fresh meat' but rather to bring it back gently and hand it over to his owner without hesitation is just awe-inspiring; what have we done to deserve such compliance and devotion?

It was this element of nature versus nurture, or inherent versus trained, that I wanted to explore for my Masters degree and so the project of "Canine cognition: Inherent versus trained behaviour in following the point" was born.

Dogs communicate to each other by means of looking at something or 'gazing' at it; they communicate to us in the same way. All you have to do is stand next to the treat jar and ask your dog what he wants and he'll look at it. Bart was a master at manipulating us through his gaze to get what he wanted; at the vets he used to sit in front of Juliet wagging his tail, then he'd look at the treat pot behind her, then back to Juliet, then back at the treat pot, wagging his tail ever faster and dancing on the spot if she headed towards it.

We also communicate with 'the gaze'; young babies will often do as Bart did, directing people's attention by looking at the object of their desire. Once we learn to point however, there's no stopping us - we point at everything.

I don't know if you did this when you were younger or not, but me and my mates did and used to have a great time doing it; we would stand in the street, or in a shopping centre and look up, then point up – the amount of people who followed our point and looked up was hysterical (we were teenagers, remember). They just couldn't resist it. And who can blame them, it's about more than being nosey, it's about survival; if way back when, we didn't respond when someone pointed at something, we could end up being eaten.

Whether we realise it or not, gazing and pointing make up such a huge part of our communication system, not just with other people, but with those that share our lives, namely our dogs.

Not long before I submitted my dissertation it was my birthday and I was standing in the kitchen with my son before he went off to school, "What no birthday card?" I asked – he let his eyes slide towards my office - in I went and there was my card on my desk. Realising what I did I rushed back into the kitchen and said to my son, "I've just followed the gaze!!!" to which he rolled his eyes and said "yes mum".

Because we use 'the point', or a form thereof, for direction control I decided I would put it to the test on trained gundogs. I organised ten gundogs that I knew were proficient in following the 'get out' command to take part in my experiment; I didn't let anyone know what we were doing, only that there was no pressure for them or their dogs to get anything 'right'.

The dogs were sat between a couple of pegs and given the 'get out' command along with either with the point, the gaze or a combination of the two (that is pointing to one side and gazing to the other); they had to cross the peg line for it to count as successfully following the command. It was absolutely fascinating.

When presented with a combination of both the gaze and the point, the same number of dogs followed the gaze as followed the point. We couldn't believe it as none of the dogs had been trained to follow the gaze on a 'get out' command.

As you've probably guessed, I've changed the way that I train the 'get out' so that as well as using the arm signal to indicate the direction to go in, I now also draw on inherent behaviour by looking in the same direction as I send the dog for the retrieve, hopefully making it easier for our dogs to understand what it is that we want them to do.

For my Masters degree I tested the gundog's ability to follow the point, and defined it as: the Point is referring to the arm extended away from the body with either an open hand or a distal point.

An example of Pointing to the right, the experiment called for the other arm to be placed behind the back and body to remain static.

I also tested the gundog's ability to follow the gaze and defined it as: The Gaze is turning the head in the direction that we are indicating the dog should follow.

An example of Gazing to the left, the experiment called for both arms to be placed behind the back and body to remain static

And the final test was a combination of both commands...

An example of Gazing to the left whilst Pointing to the right, the experiment called for the left arm to be placed behind the back and the body to remain static.

Useful contacts

The British Association for Shooting & Conservation (BASC)
www.basc.org.uk

National Organisation of Beaters and Pickers Up (NOBS)
www.nobs.org.uk

The Countryside Alliance
www.countryside-alliance.org.uk

The Kennel Club
www.thekennelclub.org.uk

The Gundog Club
www.thegundogclub.co.uk

Dog Training and Behaviour

The Cambridge Institute of Dog Behaviour & Training
www.cidbt.org.uk

The Canine & Feline Behaviour Association of Great Britain
www.cfba.co.uk

The Guild of Dog Trainers
www.godt.org.uk

Equipment

Quest Gundog Training Equipment
www.questgundogs.co.uk

Working Dog Company
www.workingdogcompany.co.uk

Hi-lost
www.hilost.co.uk

Game fairs

Countryman Fairs
www.countrymanfairs.co.uk

Living Heritage
www.livingheritagecountryshows.co.uk

Scurry Bandits
www.scurrybandits.org

Lez' sites

Lez Graham books
www.lezgraham.com

Trained for Life
www.trainedforlife.co.uk

The Pet Gundog
www.thepetgundog.co.uk

Photography

Nick Ridley Photography
www.nickridley.com